THE FIGURE OF ARTHUR
by
CHARLES WILLIAMS

British Library Cataloguing-in-Publication Data
A catalogue record for this book is available from
the British Library

CHARLES WILLIAMS

Charles Walter Stansby Williams was born in London in 1886. He dropped out of University College London in 1904, and was hired by Oxford University Press as a proof-reader, quickly rising to the position of editor. While there, arguably his greatest editorial achievement was the publication of the first major English-language edition of the works of the Danish philosopher Søren Kierkegaard.

Williams began writing in the twenties and went on to publish seven novels. Of these, the best-known are probably *War in Heaven* (1930), *Descent into Hell* (1937), and *All Hallows' Eve* (1945) – all fantasies set in the contemporary world. He also published a vast body of well-received scholarship, including a study of Dante entitled *The Figure of Beatrice* (1944) which remains a standard reference text for academics today, and a highly unconventional history of the church, *Descent of the Dove* (1939). Williams garnered a number of well-known admirers, including T. S. Eliot, W. H. Auden and C. S. Lewis. Towards the end of his life, he gave lectures at Oxford University on John Milton, and received an honorary MA degree. Williams died almost exactly at the close of World War II, aged 58.

To

MICHAL WILLIAMS

*without whose permission this book could not
have been made*

HEU QUIS TE CASUS DEIECTAM CONIUGE TANTO
EXCIPIT AUT QUAE DIGNA SATIS FORTUNA REVISIT,
HECTORIS ANDROMACHE ?

CONTENTS

THE FIGURE OF ARTHUR
by *Charles Williams*

CHAPTER I

The Beginnings

THE point at which the myth of Arthur begins does not, in its first appearance, hold any mention of the king. It does not, in fact, hold the name of a hero at all. It occurs in the pages of a treatise by a monk writing in the middle of the sixth century ; his name was Gildas, and the name of his book *De Excidio Britanniae.* The book is largely made up of exhortations to the Britons and of denunciations of their wicked kings, but these are preceded by a brief history of Britain since the coming of the Romans. He speaks of the withdrawal of the Romans, of the Saxon invasions, and of the wars between the Saxons and the Britons. The Britons were almost continuously defeated—many killed, some enslaved, some fugitives in the mountains or in exile beyond the sea—until they found a leader called Ambrosius Aurelianus. He was the descendant of a noble Roman family, but himself not notable until this crisis arose. He had some success against the Saxons, and established with them a kind of uncertain equality in the field. ' The battles ', says Gildas, ' were sometimes won by my countrymen and sometimes by the enemy.' This state of affairs lasted until the *obsessio Badonici montis*—the siege of Mount Badon. ' What was almost the last—though not the least—destruction of our cruel foes took place there.' Gildas adds that his own birth happened at this time. He mentions a period of forty-four years and one month, but scholars are divided whether this is meant to conclude in or begin from the battle. It would be convenient to the myth to suppose it the latter.

After the victory of Mount Badon, Gildas continues, the Britons, those who had known both the invasion and the victory, for some time ' lived orderly ' in their several vocations—kings, magistrates, priests, other clerics, and all the commons in general.

By the time Gildas was writing, however, another generation—some twenty or thirty years younger than he—had grown up. They had not known the danger or the deliverance, and (as younger generations are always said to do) they behaved less well. 'Laws', said Gildas in the very voice of a man of almost fifty, 'are now shaken and turned upside down, and there is no virtue anywhere.' He enlarged on this theme for the rest of his work, giving—it must be admitted—a number of horrid particulars.

We have then in Gildas a picture of the over-running of Britain by the Saxons until a rally under a leader of Roman descent holds them off, and prepares for 'the siege of Mount Badon' after which the Saxons are unable again to make head. The troubles in the time of Gildas did not arise so much from them as from civil wars between the patriots. The descendants of Ambrosius Aurelianus, degenerate as Gildas held them to be, were still capable of dealing with the pagans from beyond sea. But there is in all this no word of Arthur.

That name occurs for the first time four centuries later, and is still not that of a king. In the ninth century another monk, called Nennius, wrote a similar history, but in more detail. He gives the story of the calling in of the Saxons, under their leaders Hengist and Horsa, by the British Vortigern ; of the marriage of Vortigern to Rowena, Hengist's daughter ; of the new arrivals of Saxons in force ; of the outbreak of war and of the defeat of the Britons. He too speaks of a rally, but under a leader Vortimer ; he mentions Ambrosius later, however, as 'king among all the kings of the Britons'. The war desperately continues, until the rise of a new hero. Nennius goes on :

'Then Arthur fought with the Saxons, alongside the kings of the Britons, but he himself was the leader in the battles. The first battle was on the banks of the river which is called Gelin. The next four were on the banks of another river, which is called Dubylas and is in the region Linnius. The sixth was on a river which is called Bossa. The seventh was in the wood of Celidon ; that is, Cat Coit Celidon. The eighth was by Castle Guinnion, in which Arthur carried on his shoulders an image of St. Mary Ever-Virgin, and on that day the pagans were put to flight, and there was a great slaughter of them, through the strength of our Lord Jesus Christ and of the holy Mary His Maiden-Mother. The ninth was in the City of the Legion. The tenth was on the bank of the river which is called Tribiut. The eleventh was on the hill called Agned. The twelfth was on Mount Badon, in which—on that one day—there fell in one onslaught of Arthur's nine hundred and sixty men ; and none slew them but he alone, and in all the battles he remained victor.'

Another MS. adds that before Badon

' Arthur had gone to Jerusalem, where he had caused to be made a cross of the same size as the life-giving Cross, and after it had been consecrated he had fasted and kept vigil and prayed by it for three days together, asking that by this wood the Lord would give him victory over the pagans, which was so done. And he carried with him the image of St. Mary.'

Nennius has a few more things to say of Arthur. He records certain wonderful things of which he had heard or which he had seen in the Britain of his day ; that is, in South Wales. One is

' a marvel in the region which they call Buelt. For there is a heap of stones, and on the top of the heap one stone bearing the footprint of a dog. When they hunted the boar Troynt, Cabal which was the dog of Arthur the soldier, put his foot on that stone and marked it ; and Arthur afterwards piled up a heap of stones and that stone on top, on which was his dog's footprint, and called it Carn Cabal. And men will come and carry away that stone for a day and a night, and the next morning there it is back again on its heap.'

Another wonder is in the district called Ercing.

' There is a burial mound near a spring which is known as Licat Anir, and the name of the man who is buried in the mound was called Anir. He was the son of the soldier Arthur, and Arthur himself killed him there and buried him. And when men come to measure the length of the mound, they find it sometimes six feet, sometimes nine, sometimes twelve, and sometimes fifteen. Whatever length you find it at one time, you will find it different at another, and I myself have proved this to be true.'

(The last statement is one of those mind-shattering things one finds in history. 'Et ego solus probavi.' Nennius has been careful enough all through to say that 'it is said' or 'which is called'. He says nothing about proving the tale of the stone. And then, as it were unnecessarily, he dares his reader to disbelieve him on this one point. Was the sentence added later? Was he, suddenly and wildly, a liar? Was there some simple, but obscure, explanation? Or was there something very odd about that burial-ground?)

Another document, a century later than Nennius, the *Annales Cambriae*, has two entries, in the second of which is an additional statement about Arthur. The entries are:

' 518 : The battle of Badon in which Arthur carried the cross of our Lord Jesus Christ, for three days and three nights, on his shoulders, and the Britons were the victors.

' 549 : The battle of Camlaun in which Arthur and Medraut were slain ; and there was death in England and Ireland.'

These are the early records or appearances of record. The fact that Gildas does not mention Arthur was attributed in the twelfth century to a personal—or rather a family—enmity. The brother of Gildas was said to have been killed by Arthur in a feud, and it was added that Gildas wrote as he did about the kings of Britain because of this killing, and that he had thrown into the sea 'those books in which he had written of the deeds of Arthur and his countrymen'. This is why there is in his work no authentic history of the king. But by this time the myth had begun to come seriously into being, and it was as necessary to explain the apparent omissions as to invent occasional allusions. It is certain that Gildas does not mention him ; we cannot certainly say whether this was because he was at feud with him, or because he did not know of him, or because there had never been any Arthur for him to know.

History, however, has of late inclined to let us believe in the reality of Arthur. The late R. G. Collingwood, in the first volume of the *Oxford History of England*, put forward a convincing suggestion. He argued that the evidence we have of his battles becomes clear as soon as we ' envisage Arthur as the commander of a mobile field-army'. At that period the Roman High Command was, in its European wars, using cavalry to a greater and greater extent. ' The late Empire was in fact the age which established the ascendancy of heavy cavalry, clothed in chain-mail, over infantry. Already in the first twenty years of the century the count of Britain commanded six regiments of cavalry to three of infantry, and anyone thereafter, reviving his office with some knowledge of what it implied, would know that a count of Britain should be a cavalry general.' Professor Collingwood went on to point out that, even without this special intention, a very small experience of contemporary warfare would expose the advantage of a mounted force. The local levies, defending particular towns, would have none. The highland tribes had none. The Saxon invaders certainly had none, just as they had no body-armour, and very little tactical cohesion. ' Any one who could enrol on his own initiative a band of mail-clad cavalry, using as mounts the ordinary horses of the lowland zone and relying for armament on the standard work of contemporary smiths, and could persuade the British kings of their value, might have done what Arthur is said to have done.' The list of battles in Nennius suggests that his mobile field-army moved, as it could do, all over the country, and was able to strike at different places. The final crashing victory at Mount Badon may mean that the Saxons had at last managed to confine this force to ' some British hill-fort, reconditioned, as Cissbury was, for defence against the invaders '. The phrases describing it— ' one onslaught of Arthur's', ' none but he alone '—may suggest that in this last battle he was not supporting some local king, but operating solely with his own force.

The site of Badon cannot be fixed. It has been supposed to be on a line of British earthworks running from the Bristol Channel to the Marlborough Downs near Newbury. It has been identified with Bath, with Badbury Ring, with other Badburys, with Bedwyn, with Baydon, Beedon, Bowdon, and

Bown Hill. All is very doubtful ; on the whole, Liddington Hill, which has a Badbury near it, and might threaten a Saxon advance to the West, seems as good a guess as any and better than some.

We have then, to put all together, at least a possibility, behind the chronicles and the hypotheses—and perhaps rather more than a possibility—of an historic figure. The Saxon invaders, after a period of almost complete victory, had been checked by a chieftain, local but still notable among the British chiefs, of Romano-British descent. For some time after his success, the war hung level. There then came into prominence a man with a capacity for seeing and seizing military advantages. His name was Arthur ; he too may have been of Roman descent, since the name Arturus belongs to a Roman *gens*. He raised a force of mounted men, and went to the aid of the kings, when and how the military situation required. Eventually the Saxons were compelled to make an advance in strength into the west. The Captain-General took up a position on a fortified hill threatening this advance. The enemy besieged, or attempted to besiege, this hill. They were defeated, and wholly routed by a final cavalry charge led by Arthur himself. The result of the battle was that they retired to their own part of the country, and that for thirty or forty years the Britons were left in comparative peace, under the prestige of the Captain-General. During the earlier part of that time, the organizations of their State (or States) operated freely and effectively. But afterwards disputes and wars broke out among them, in one of which Arthur was killed. The cavalry, after this, either no longer existed or had no adequate leader. The Saxons renewed their attacks ; the divided and warring Britons could put up no sufficient defence ; and presently the invaders subdued and occupied the whole country except the extreme West. But the memory, and indeed the name, of Arthur still remained as a fable of the past and a prophecy of the future.

It was, however, by no means certain that that name would last, still less that it would enter into a great literature. It might have faded under the Saxons, let alone under the Normans. It was not to fade, and the time of decision was the twelfth century. Up to then Tennyson's later lines describe the situation not inaptly :

> that grey king whose name, a ghost,
> Streams like a cloud, man-shaped, from mountain peak,
> And cleaves to cairn and cromlech still.

Many names, so streaming, have not been re-imaged in poetry or even convincing prose. This name seems first to have been raised to royalty about 1075 (as far as our records go), in a *Legenda Sancti Goeznovii*, or rather in the historical prelude to the life of the saint. There the pride of the Saxons (' pagans and devilish men '—soon after the Norman Conquest) is crushed ' per magnum Arturum Britonum regem ', a precursor, as it were, of the Conqueror. Arthur proceeds to win other victories in Gaul as well as in Britain, after which, he having been ' ab humanis actibus evocato ', the Saxons return. The phrasing is of some interest ; the King is called away from human activity ; he is not absolutely said to have died. It was still about this time currently reported by some of the poor who knew and repeated the name that he was to return. There is a tale, of about 1146, recounting events of 1113, which shows this. The canons of Laon, wishing to rebuild their cathedral, sent some of their number to England to raise funds, taking with them certain relics of Our Lady of Laon. They came to Devonshire ; they heard of the tales of the Britons concerning ' the famous King Arthur '. At Bodmin a man with a withered arm came to be healed by the holy relics. He and one of the visitors—Haganellus, related to the lord Guy, archdeacon of Laon—fell into a dispute. The man with the withered arm maintained that Arthur still lived ; it seems likely, though we have no details, that the archdeacon's relative told him not to be such a fool. There was a demonstration in force by the man's friends ; they rushed into the church ' cum armis ', and there would have been bloodshed if a cleric named Algard had not somehow managed to interfere. It was clearly felt in Bodmin that foreigners had no business to sneer at local tradition. But the foreigners had the last victory. Our Lady of Laon was displeased ; and ' the man who had the withered arm, who had caused the tumult on behalf of Arthur, was not healed '.

The man made such trouble ' as the Britons make with the French about King Arthur ', the chronicle says. The Britons are, no doubt, the Bretons, and it follows that the tale was already widely known in that part of Europe. But it had—or certain names had—spread even more widely.

CHAPTER II

The Grail

THE point at which the myth of the Grail begins holds in its first appearance the most important account of all. No invention can come near it; no fabulous imagination excel it. All the greatest mythical details are only there to hint at the thing which happens; that which in the knowledge of Christendom is the unifying act, perilous and perpetual, universal and individual. That origin took place in the Jerusalem to which (it was reported) the Captain-General Arthur had gone before his final victory. Its record is in the Gospels; it is taken here from the Revised Version of the Gospel of St. Mark.

'And as they were eating he [Jesus] took bread, and when he had blessed, he brake it, and gave it to them, and said, Take ye : this is my body, and he took a cup, and when he had given thanks, he gave it to them : and they all drank of it. And he said unto them, This is my blood of the covenant, which is shed for many. Verily I say unto you, I will no more drink of the fruit of the vine, until that day when I drink it new in the kingdom of God.'

This is the first mention of that Cup which in its progress through the imagination of Europe was to absorb into itself so many cauldrons of plenty and vessels of magic.

It was not for some centuries that the intellectual attention of Christendom directed itself to the nature of the Blessed Sacrament. Its first preoccupation was with the nature of God and of the Redeemer. Piety and spiritual devotion might centre on it, but the lesser powers of the Church (so to call them) were not yet free to turn to it. The identification in some sense of the Eucharist with our Lord was immediate ; the documents of the New Testament confirmed, when they came, the settled habit of the Church. It was regarded as a sacrifice—by Christ and of Christ ; therefore, as a sacerdotal act. It was used, as well it might be, as an argument against the Gnostic doctrines of the unreality of matter and of the evil of the flesh. The sense in which the dedicated elements were consecrated into something other was not defined. Nor the moment of change ; our Lord was supposed by some to condescend to the whole Rite and general prayer of the Church ; by others, to the actual repetition of the Words of Institution. But on these things there was as yet no controversy.

Only the Act continued everywhere. The phrase of the New Testament—' He was known of them in the breaking of bread ' —remained true and became more widely true, although the knowledge was not intellectually epigrammatized. The relation of the elements to the Sacred Body was called sometimes identity, sometimes figure or symbol. But neither figure nor symbol implied separation ; each word implied an interior closeness which they have perhaps with us lost. The Act was priestly, by Christ and for Christ ; the mysterious sacrifice was of Christ ; and Christ in it was the food of man. The sacrifice was offered not only on earth but in the heights of the heavens. He offered, who was the offering, and there was as yet no controversy in the Church.

But as the Nature of our Lord was defined, and as the Church became more and more aware of what in fact she believed, so the intellectual problems of that Act were more and more discussed. It was stressed now one way and now another ; but no stress necessarily denied another. It was a symbol, but it was He. It was the offering of His passion, and communion with His ascended life ; also it was communion with His passion and an offering of His ascended life. This was His very death ; it was also His very Resurrection ; it was, all ways, His Incarnation. It was a double Act ; there was a kind of exchange in it. The Church gave itself, and Christ gave Himself, and the two were united. ' If you have received well ', said Augustine, ' you are that which you have received.' Such a sentence, in some sense, holds all ; it is this which, in the English words of

Malory, centuries later, was 'the secret of our Lord Jesus Christ'.

It was this communion which was referred to in the Lord's Prayer. St. Cyril of Jerusalem wrote : ' *Give us this day our substantial bread :* Common bread is not substantial, but this holy bread is substantial. . . . It is imparted to your whole system for the benefit of body and soul.' [1] And as it was communicated for each body and soul, so it was all bodies and souls in the Church that were offered. ' The whole redeemed City itself is offered as a universal sacrifice to God by the High Priest ', wrote St. Augustine. ' In a certain sense ', he wrote again about the first Institution, ' He carried Himself in His hands.' This was the centre of the Christian and Catholic life : ' in this thing which the Church offers she herself is offered.'

So the great meditations ran on. There were—not so much disputes as faint disagreements, but there still seems to have been very little controversy. In East and West alike the sense of the Act grew keener ; the belief in the identification of the elements with Christ clearer. Miraculous visions began to appear —as in the tale in the *Paradise of the Fathers* (meaning the hermits of the Thebaid) in which an angel is seen slaying a child with a knife. The child or the man was seen ' smiting itself into the bread '. And with the visions, the controversies ; the young Church had known neither.

They did not however seriously begin in the West until about the eleventh century. No more need be said of them here than may suggest how the subject exercised the minds of men ; how therefore it preoccupied their minds. This is not to say that it was argued about in every place where men talked. But it was very likely to be at least spoken—if not argued—about in any place where the intellectuals talked. It was not, I suppose, dis-

[1] Quoted in *A History of the Doctrine of the Holy Eucharist* : Darwell Stone ; from which the other quotations are taken—C. W. [Beside this footnote Williams has pencilled ' Tolkien '. This means that Professor Tolkien here raised some philological questions about the meaning of ἐπιούσιον (Matt. vi. 11) and, probably that Williams intended to discuss the matter with him more fully on some later occasion—C. S. L.]

cussed as politics are to-day, but neither was its discussion con-
fined to a particular class of the pious, as such things usually are
to-day. A more general imagination, a more universal (almost
—dare one say ?—a more *casual*) intellect was aware of it ; and
even the people who did not argue had probably heard of the
argument. For something like two centuries the nature of that
Act and of its consequences was, in various times and places,
disputed. Decisions were taken by Councils ; rites were
ordained by bishops ; devotions were multiplied by the pious.
So that, slowly perhaps but generally, among all the other
affairs of secular and religious life, the image of that Act, and of
the Host and the Chalice which were its means, grew primary in
the imagination of Europe.

A few points in that development may be mentioned. About
1040 Berengar of Tours, Archdeacon of Angers, was believed to
have taught that the Body in the Mystery was not to be identified
with that which was born of our Lady St. Mary, and to have
denied any ' conversion ' of the elements. He was opposed by,
among others, Lanfranc, afterwards Archbishop of Canterbury ;
who, in maintaining the reality of that conversion, declared that
the many occasions on which the body of Christ had been
miraculously seen in the Sacrament, proved the reality of the
presence. Durand, Abbot of Troarn, wrote that the Sacrament
was ' none other than that very flesh which the Virgin conceived
of the Holy Ghost, and brought forth with the integrity of her
spotless virginity unbroken, contrary indeed to the common
course of human nature, but not contrary to the reality of the
human body '. It is this sentence, and others like it, which
condition and characterize, as we shall see, the later image of
Galahad. The errors of Berengar were condemned at various
councils—in 1050 at Brienne (convoked by William of Normandy, afterwards William I of England, and patron of Lanfranc), in 1059 in Rome, in 1063 at Rouen, and in 1078 and 1079
again at Rome under the presidency of Gregory VII. At all of
these the doctrine of the identification was asserted, and ' the
union of flesh and soul in the resurrection of Christ '. The

phrase is ascribed to St. Peter Damian (1007–1072).[1] To him also is ascribed in the West the first use of the word *transubstantiation*.

A few other phrases from the end of the eleventh or beginning of the twelfth century may be quoted, to show the kind of doctrine and of image that was in the heart and the imagination of Christendom. Odo of Cambrai (1050–1113) wrote : ' It is divided and it cannot be consumed. It is eaten, but it remains uncorrupted. It is crushed and it is unimpaired. It is broken, and it is whole. This offering is flesh, but it is not carnal. It is unstained light rather, and pure. It is body, but not corporal. It is spiritual light rather, and pure. It is pure and cleansing, pure and purifying, pure because divine, more pure than material light.' And again : ' It is offered here, it is accepted there, not by change of place or succession of time, as if a movement of translation were begun in one place and completed in another. . . . There is no transference of place that bread may become flesh yet there is transference from the altar to heaven, because from being bread it is made God. . . . The Word of God is the altar on high.' Honorius of Autun (d. 1130) wrote : ' This is the same thing in the mouth of the worst of men as it is in the mouth of the most holy. . . . But, as the sun is the same in its heat and in its brightness, and yet produces different results in these two aspects, namely, burning the earth by its heat and giving light by its brightness, so the flesh of Christ remaining the same produces different results in different persons, incorporating the righteous with himself, separating the unrighteous from his life.' Robert Paululus (*c.* 1178) wrote : ' The golden altar [in the Jewish Tabernacle] signifies the altar of faith in the heart that is purged by penitence, and bright and clear with the testimony of a good conscience. On this altar the priest, now dead to the world but living to God, no longer the old Melchizedeck, flesh born of flesh, but the new man, spirit born of spirit, offers the invisible offering of flesh and blood through the oblation of earthly food.' Rupert of Deutz (d. 1135) wrote : ' Because the

---

[1] The MS. here gives a blank place enclosed in brackets.—C. S. L.

A.T.   C

13

Virgin conceived him of the Holy Ghost, who is eternal fire, and he himself through the same Holy Ghost, as the Apostle says, offered himself a living sacrifice to the living God, by the same fire is the roasting (" roast with fire "—that is, burnt by the travail of the Passion) on the altar, for by the operation of the Holy Ghost the bread becomes the body and the wine the blood of Christ.' William of Champeaux (d. 1121) defined the ' doctrine of concomitance ' in the phrase : ' He who receives either species receives the whole Christ. . . . In each species is the whole Christ, who after his resurrection is wholly invisible and impassible and indivisible, so that neither is the blood without the flesh, nor the flesh without the blood, nor either without the human soul, nor the whole human nature without the Word of God personally united to it.' Hildebert of Tours (1057–1134) defined the method of the Act : ' I utter the words of the Canon and the Word of the Transubstantiation.' And, as a final quotation, as if peculiarly applicable to that great myth which was soon to come into being, as if it were a warning and a watchword to the poets and makers of romances, Ivo of Chartres (1040–1116) declared in a sermon : ' It is a sacrament of faith ; search can be made into it healthfully, but not without danger '.

The climax of all this followed in the early years of the thirteenth century. Lothair Conti (1160–1216) became Pope under the title of Innocent III in 1198. Before his elevation to the Pontificate, he had written a book *On the Holy Mystery of the Altar*. He defines there ' the double sense of the four kinds of altars, whereby the " higher altars " denotes the Holy Trinity and the Church Triumphant, the " lower altar " the Church Militant and the " Table of the Temple ", the " inner altar " a clean heart and faith in the Incarnation, the " outward altar " the altar of the Cross and the Sacraments of the Church '. The offering is made not by the priest in his own person but in the person of the whole Church. ' The offering is primarily directed to God the Father as the first principle of the Godhead, yet the sacrifice of praise is offered equally to the Undivided Trinity.' The risen Body, thus communicated, has four qualities which were manifested in the Body before the resurrection : ' subtlety (when He was born of the Virgin), glory (when He was transfigured on the mount), agility (when He walked on the sea), impassibility (when He was eaten at the Supper).' ' By the power of this Sacrament it becomes possible that they who are of earth ascend to heaven.'.

After his accession, Innocent prepared for what was one of the greatest Councils of the Middle Ages. It was held in the Lateran, in the year 1215. More than four hundred bishops, twice as many abbots and priors, many representatives of kings and princes were there. The Albigensian ' crusade ' had ended just before. It had been a dreadful and murderous business. But its cruelties must not prevent the recognition of the nature of the war, so far as it can now be discerned. It seems probable that there had grown up in Provence a kind of culture deriving from the old Gnostic dreams. Matter was either evil or negligible ; it was irrelevant to salvation and incapable of it. The adept would be—perhaps was already—free from it. It was directly against this doctrine that St. Dominic preached and Innocent sent the armies ; and against it, less directly and more universally, that the first chapter of the decrees ' On the Catholic Faith ' was proclaimed. It decreed :

' There is one universal Church of the faithful, outside which no one at all is in a state of salvation. In this Church Jesus Christ himself is both priest and sacrifice ; and his body and blood are really contained in the sacrament of the altar under the species of bread and wine, the bread being transubstantiated into the body and the wine into the blood by the power of God, so that, to effect the mystery of unity, we ourselves receive of that which is His, what He Himself received of that which is ours.'

By this decree the doctrine of the Eucharist was, as it were, raised to the level of the great formulating doctrines. It was, formally and theologically, received among those dogmas which defined the Triune Nature of the Omnipotence and the Double Nature of the Redeemer. But between those other doctrines and this, there was one extreme difference. All were ' of faith ', but in those others the faith was directed towards the Invisible and in this towards the visible. The Triune Omnipotence, the Two-Natured Redeemer, were real but (since His Ascension) removed. But the transubstantiating Body was visible in the transubstantiated matter of the elements—real and unremoved. There, visible but hidden, perfect under either species, were the subtlety, the glory, the agility, the impassibility. They were there for sacrifice and for communion. The true Priest (hidden in wafer and in wine) offered them, and generously permitted the Church and City a participation in His Act.

The theology was accompanied by the ordering of ritual. Decorum was enjoined on physical movement, as it was on intellectual development ; proper order was to rule in all. In the eleventh century at Canterbury Lanfranc had taken care of this, as he had earlier defended the Identity. He directed the method of the sacramental processions on Palm Sunday and the order of the genuflections. The abbot Simon of St. Albans followed him in the next century. It was to St. Albans that the King Henry II Plantagenet (whose name, one way or another, is so commingled with the Matter of Britain) sent a most costly cup to hold ' the case immediately containing the Body of Christ '. At Paris and at Cologne, at Salisbury and at Oxford, in Ireland and at Rome, from popes, bishops, and synods, decrees of order issued. The ringing of a bell at the consecration, and at the same time kneeling or prostration, intercessions and adorations, were placed and timed. The *Ancren Riwle* and the *Lay Folks' Mass Book* contain similar instuctions. In the first (dated in the early part of the thirteenth century) the anchoresses for whom it was meant are instructed, when they are dressed in the morning, ' to think upon God's flesh and on His blood, which is over the high altar, and fall on your knees towards it, with this salutation : " Hail, Author of our creation ! Hail, Price of our Redemption ! Hail, Support of our Pilgrimage ! Hail, Reward of our expectation ! " '

There was, in that century and after Lateran, one more grand development, which was hagiologically referred to the initiative

of Christ Himself. Such an initiative was indeed (it is a point
to be remembered, whether in the theology or in the myth) at
the root of the whole matter. It was our Lord who had first
acted and who continued to act. It is this which dominates the
fables and inventions : all of them are subject to and conditioned
by this. Galahad is conditioned by this. The whole Act is
Christ's and is imparted to those who are also His. But now, as
he had commenced the Act, and indoctrinated the theology, He
was said to have directed the ritual. A Belgian nun named
Juliana was a devotee of the Sacrament. Soon after Lateran,
she had a vision of a full moon, in which was one black spot.
She became aware that this appearance exhibited the lack in the
liturgical year of any feast in honour of the Sacred Body. Her
vision was communicated to the then Bishop of Liége, who in
1246 bade a feast of Corpus Christi be held in his diocese. In
1264 the Pope Urban IV, who had once been Archdeacon of
Liége, by the Bull *Transiturus* commanded it to be observed
through the whole of the Western Church. It could not be
fixed for the day of Institution, the Thursday of Holy Week,
because then the Church ' is not able to be fully at leisure for the
commemoration of this chief Sacrament'. ' Therefore, to confirm and exalt the Catholic Faith, we have worthily and reasonably determined to appoint that, concerning so great a Sacrament,
besides the daily memorial which the Church makes of it, there
be celebrated yearly a more solemn and special memorial,
appointing for this purpose a fixed day, namely, the Thursday
after the Octave of Pentecost. . . . We exhort and command . . .
that you keep so great and glorious a feast every year on the
aforesaid Thursday with devotion and solemnity.' For this new
feast, at the request and by the command of the Pope, St. Thomas
Aquinas composed the Office and the great hymn *Pange, lingua,
gloriosi*, and (though not for the Office) ' Devoutly I adore thee '.
 Such then, in brief summary, was the development of Doctrine.
The Act had gathered into itself all circumstances. It had, as
it were, sunk into, and now dwelled among, all the most funda-
mental dogmas. It united all contraries in a mystery of exchange.

The Flesh and the Blood, invoked by the act of the celebrant, were there in their own full act—and were yet passive. They were carried, and were unmoving ; they were eaten, yet they themselves received the eater into themselves ; they were separate, yet they were one. They were the visibility of the invisible. They were the material centre of Christendom ; and they were the very Act that made them so.

The doctrinal intellect had so defined them. The general imagination, having helped that definition, now received it. But in the period, at least, before Lateran, the circumstances of the Act were received more generally than perhaps they afterwards came to be. Almost any article connected with the Act served for its symbol. Paten or cup, monstrance or tabernacle, were alike used. The word Grail itself is defined by the dictionaries as coming from the Latin *gradalis* and meaning a shallow dish ; thus, the paten ; and afterwards, erroneously, the cup. But the ' erroneously ' is hardly justified. The Grail may, etymologically, have been a dish. In the poems and romances it was ' chose espirituel '. Even in the Rites there were similarities between the objects used. ' In the Middle Ages there was not a clear distinction in form nor in part (from doctrinal motives) even in function between the vessel that contained the wine in the Eucharist, and the one that contained the holy wafer. The latter, as well as the former, had the shape of a cup, as it still has in the Catholic Church of to-day, and it was also not infrequently called the " chalice " (*calix*)—indeed, down into the eighteenth century.' [1] ' In the eleventh century, the host was broken on the paten, but in the twelfth century Durandus directs that it be broken over the chalice.' [2] The various actions of the Rite were to be accommodated, as far as might be, to the sense of the whole Christ. He was whole under each species— double but undivided, and the Rite was to exhibit him so.

Something perhaps should be said—and may be said here as

[1] J. D. Bruce : *The Evolution of Arthurian Romance.* 1928.
[2] Lizette A. Fisher : *The Mystic Vision in the Grail Legend and in the Divine Comedy.* 1917.

well as anywhere—about those fabulous vessels, which from
Celtic or whatever sources, emerged into general knowledge.
There has been much controversy about them—vessels of plenty
and cauldrons of magic—and they have been supposed by
learned experts to be the origin of the Grail myth. That, in the
Scriptural and ecclesiastical sense, they certainly cannot be.
Cup or dish or container of whatever kind, the Grail in its
origin entered Europe with the Christian and Catholic Faith.
It came from and with Christ, and it came with and from no one
else. The Eucharist, in Europe, was earlier than any evidence
of the fables ; that is a matter of history. But then it is a matter
of history also that the Eucharist, as it came from and with
the whole Christ, was meant for the whole man. It was for
his eternal salvation, body and soul ; and the doctrinal development precisely stressed this. It was therefore, in the very idea
of it, greater than any vessel of less intention could possibly be.
If it swallowed up its lesser rivals, it did so exactly because it was
greater. The poetic inventiveness of Europe found itself presented with the image of a vessel much more satisfying to it—
merely as an image—than any other. There is no need to suppose the poets and romancers were particularly devout ; it is
only necessary to suppose they were good poets and real
romancers. A dogmatic anti-Christian opposition would, no
doubt, have rejected the Grail image. But it is hard to see what
else could. Cauldrons of magic—' dire chimaeras and enchanted isles '—are all very well at first, but maturing poetry
desires something more. It desires something more actual to
existence as we know it. But the Grail contained the very
Act which was related to all that existence. Of course, it
absorbed or excluded all else ; *sui generis*, it shone alone.

CHAPTER III

The Coming of the King

I

IN the twelfth century the shape of the new metaphysical civilization of Europe was becoming clear. Traffic had been eased ; the Universities established ; kingdoms and republics settled. Communication, physical and intellectual, was more convenient than it had been for centuries. Doctrines could be contrasted and corrected ; tales compared and continued. Men began again to know what other men at a distance had said and done, and were saying and doing. No doubt this had been [1] to an extent, perhaps to a great extent, during the earlier centuries. The Dark Ages were not so dark as to blot out all. But then their light was, at best, somewhat accidental and occasional ; now it can be prolonged and intentional. The courts begin to glow with colour ; dance, in every sense, has time to return.

Certainly that dance, of whatever kind, was permitted only within general intellectual limits, but at first the limits were fairly broad. The early Middle Ages are founded on meta-physics, but they are hardly as yet built up into metaphysics. That comes about only when the profession of belief—though not, of course, belief, for of that there can be no surety—was enforced by law and power. The old Roman Empire had been based on a similar profession of belief. The incense dropped on the altars before the images of the serene and salutary Emperor meant something. But it almost flagrantly did not mean precisely what it professed to mean. The incense swung before the new altars did. Few in the old Empire can ever have been seriously challenged on the exact way in which they believed

[1] I think Williams probably meant to write *been so*, but I am not certain and therefore preserve the MS. reading.—C. S. L.

the Emperor to be divine ; but any in the new order might be at least questioned about his beliefs on Christ's.[1] No doubt, in practice, the two things were not so unlike. It would not have done to be publicly blasphemous about the Emperor, and it is certain that there must have been a good deal of scepticism in the twelfth century. Men are not so made, as far as we have yet seen, that they can lose, over a continent and for centuries, the quality of disbelief. But the social tendencies were, on the whole, towards intellectual laxity and intellectual severity respectively. A conformity of thought and practice was desired and intended by a now highly organized institution. This intention was now carried and communicated by the new easing of traffic ; and more and more, as time went on, the absence of conformity was either corrected in the confessional or penalized by the laws. The old Empire had, on the whole and except for that one important point of loyalty, left a man to think for himself, and did not much feel it mattered what he thought. The new Church felt that it mattered a good deal what he thought and consequently did not wish to leave him to think for himself. In 1184—before this very century was out—the Pope Lucius III declared the criminal nature of heresy ; in 1215 Lateran defined the Faith ; in 1233 the Inquisition was established ; in 1252 the use of torture was permitted. In this horror the formalizing of the Middle Ages came into full being.

The earlier century had had a quality of its own. It was still ' rash with theories of the right That stretched but did not break its creed '. It was still free to use its imagination in ways which would afterwards be checked or darkened or even elucidated—for example, courtly love, witchcraft, and the Holy Eucharist. All of these had their effect on the Arthurian myth. But the most important thing for the myth in that century was that it was then first seriously shaped. Geoffrey of Monmouth was born, and wrote the *Historia Regum Britanniae*. ' No work of imagination,' says Sir Edmund Chambers, ' save the *Aeneid*,

---

[1] If the sentence had been revised the first half would have ended *in the Emperor's divinity.*—C. S. L.

has done more to shape the legend of a people than the *Historia Regum Britanniae*.'

Very little is known of Geoffrey, though at that something more than of his successor in the tradition who invented Galahad. This is as it should be ; the discoverer of the King of Britain can be praised as the discoverer of the High Prince cannot be. The date of his birth is not known, but it must have been well before 1129 when he was a witness to a charter. He took priest's orders in 1152, was made Bishop of St. Asaph, and died (it is said, at mass) in 1154. He wrote two books, and by general ascription one more. The first was the *Prophecies of Merlin* (   ) ; the second was the *Historia* ; the third was a *Vita Merlini* (   ).[1]

His own account is that he had begun the *Historia* when he was asked by his ecclesiastical patron, Alexander, Bishop of Lincoln, and by others, to furnish them with a translation of the British text of Merlin's prophecies. This he did and published it. He then returned to the *Historia*, into which he inserted as a complete chapter the earlier book. The question of Merlin may be, for the moment, postponed. The *Historia* begins with the fable of the coming of the Trojan Brutus to Britain, and ends with the conquest of the country by the Saxons, or rather (after that) with the fore-telling by an angel to the last of the British kings that the Britons shall again reconquer the land ' at the time of which Merlin prophesied to Arthur '.

It was, in fact, Geoffrey's own book which was the first Return, and new conquest, of Arthur. The name, and the names of some of his companions and lords, had been widely enough spread. But now the tale suddenly grew into more than a fable ; it became a fashion. He seems to have meant to create, among his other *historiae*, one splendid and popular figure, and he seems to have succeeded. It might have happened without him, but it did happen through him. He first—and if he were not the first, yet he was the first to do it for the courts, the authors, and the reciters of Western Europe—he first made Arthur a king.

[1] Two gaps between brackets in the MS. I have not been able to discover the dates. Not all agree that Geoffrey was the author of the *Vita*.—C. S. L.

He gave him magnificence and a court. The grey tales suddenly became a diagram of glory. The dim Captain-General of Britain was changed into a champion of splendour. It is in that shape that he now lives or dies.

The ' History ' begins with the successes of Aurelius Ambrosius and his brother Uther over the Saxons. Aurelius is rebuilding cities and churches, and especially London, ' a city that had not escaped the fury of the enemy ', when he is assassinated by a Saxon. Uther succeeds him. There appears in the sky a comet the tail of which is in the shape of a dragon, and from the dragon's mouth emerge two rays of light, one directed towards Gaul, the other towards Ireland. The dragon and one ray are interpreted by Merlin to mean Uther's son Arthur and his conquests ; the other to mean his daughter, Arthur's sister. Uther, in memory and premonition, causes two golden dragons to be made, one of which is set up in the cathedral church of Winchester and the other carried about with the army.

The first story of the birth of Arthur follows—one of the then popular stories of ' magic and mystery '. Uther held a great feast in London in order ' to put on his crown ' : publicly to manifest his royalty. He was attended by his lords, among whom is Gorlois, Duke of Cornwall, and his wife Igerna. The king immediately fell deeply in love with Igerna and so markedly exhibited his love before all the court that the infuriated Gorlois withdrew from the court to his duchy, where he shut up his wife in the castle of Tintagel and himself in Dimilion. There he was besieged by Uther. But love was too strong for the king to await the result of the siege ; he complained to his friend Ulfin of how near he was to death and on his counsel had recourse to Merlin. Merlin, ' by his arts and achievements ', creates one of those grand substitutions which are very old in myth but were, in the developing tale, to find presently a wholly new significance when Lancelot came to the little castle of [Case][1] beyond Carbonek. The wizard's arts turn Uther, Ulfin, and himself into the physical

[1] The M.S. here leaves a blank space. I have supplied the name from Malory XI. ii.—C.S.L.

likeness of Gorlois and two of his companions. So changed, but so still themselves, they came in the evening to Tintagel, surrounded on all sides but one by sea, and on that having a mass of rock with but one narrow entrance. There, ' in the evening twilight ', Uther, wearing the appearance of the Duke, was admitted. He protested to the Duchess Igerna that he had left his other castle only from love of her and only for a single night ; and she, believing and his wife, ' never thought to refuse him anything '. On that night ' the most renowned Arthur ' is conceived. In the morning new messages from Dimilion arrived, this time real and true ; to bring news that Uther—or rather his army—had stormed the castle and that Gorlois was dead. They stood before the seeming Gorlois, bewildered and blushing with astonished shame. He, sitting by Igerna, declared that he would make peace with the king. He rode out, put off the magical likeness, became Uther again, stormed Tintagel, and eventually married Igerna. They lived ' in no small love ', and besides Arthur had one other child, the princess Anne. Uther in the end dies while encamped at Verulam, through drinking from ' a spring of very clear water ', which has been poisoned by the Saxons.

All this forms the eighth book of the *Historia*. The ninth is given up to Arthur. He was recognized as Uther's son by the lords, and crowned by Dubricius, Archbishop of the City of the Legions, Caerleon, at the age of fifteen. He was then ' a youth of such peculiar courage and generosity, of such a sweet temper and instructive[1] goodness, that he is greatly loved by all the people '. He was, in fact, at an earlier age, much like Shakespeare's Henry V, and his subsequent actions are not at all dissimilar. The Saxons were still in control of half the country, and Arthur determined to make war on them, because (i) he wished to enrich his own followers with their wealth, (ii) that wealth, and the whole country, was his by right. The two are

---

[1] Thus the MS. The Latin is *innata bonitas*. That Williams wrote or meant to write ' instinctive ' seems probable ; but not so certain as to justify emendation.—C. S. L.

not to be separated, and one might add a third, which is merely self-defence, since the Saxons are set on exterminating the whole British race. There is no need to go into details of the campaigns, in which Geoffrey's own military invention describes some, but not all, of the battles given in Nennius. Duglas is there, and the Wood of Celidon, and Badon ; others are at York, Lincoln, and Thanet, besides three in North Britain, and one by Loch Lomond against the Saxons' Irish allies.

Britain thus liberated, the king proceeded to reduce Ireland and Iceland. The kings of Gothland and of the Orkneys submitted. Here the first period of conquest ceased, and the king reigned in peace for twelve years. His court became the centre of glory and fashion—fashion in every sense of the word. Geoffrey relates that not only did King Arthur introduce such high courtesy as was imitated in the manners of the most distant lands, but that no lord in the world thought himself of any worth unless his arms and clothes were made in the same style as those of the lords of King Arthur. Those lords are not, on the whole, those whom we later know, but three names are familiar. There is Lot, who is then the nephew of the king of Norway, and ' consul of Londonesia ', a mature man, wise and valiant, to whom by Uther's choice Arthur's sister Anne had been married. He had two children by her, Wolgan and Modred. The other two lords who survived in later romances were Caius the king's steward, and Bedver his brother—afterwards Kay and Bedivere.

During this period of peace the king married. His wife was Guenhumara, descended from a noble Roman family, and (inevitably and properly) the most beautiful woman in Britain. But the peace did not last. All the kings of Europe became terrified of Arthur, however their lords might copy his in dress and manners. They began to make preparation against what our simpler age would call his ' aggressiveness '. Geoffrey, however, seems entirely to approve his hero, whom he causes to be full of delight at this fear, and to develop a design to conquer Europe. One cannot wholly separate this design from its final outcome in Arthur's death, but neither can one attach any serious moral value to it. Geoffrey is not writing in those terms. Arthur, according to him, began by conquering Norway, to which his brother-in-law had a kind of claim by the dead king's nomination. When Norway and Dacia had been reduced, Arthur proceeded to Gaul. This was a more serious matter, for Gaul was under the government of Flollo, a Roman tribune, who held it from the Emperor Leo, as the city of Rome itself is held in the same way by the procurator Lucius Tiberius. The seat of the imperial power in Byzantium is not mentioned ; the king is to be concerned with the west. By Geoffrey's day, of course, the Empire was divided, and yet still theoretically one. But it was as if he had enough historic sense to remember that in his Arthur's own supposedly historic day, it was not so. The king is not allowed to make war on the Emperor himself.

The tale relates how Arthur killed Flollo in single combat, occupied Gaul, and returned to Britain. There he held at Pentecost in the City of Legions a great solemnity. It is the climax and spectacle of his civil glory, though there are to be other military achievements. Caerleon was a noble city ; kings from all parts of the world came sailing to it up the Severn. In it were two marvellous churches—St. Julius, to which a nunnery was attached which served it with a choir of virgins, and St. Aaron, to which belonged a convent of canons. The city was also renowned for a college of two hundred philosophers, learned in all the arts, who astrologically divined the future and made predictions to the king. The Archbishop of the City of Legions, Dubricius, was Primate of England and Legate of the Apostolic See ; he was so holy that he could heal any sick person by his prayers. In this half-miraculous glory, the king, in the presence of all subordinate kings, consuls, and lords this side of Spain, was solemnly crowned and robed, in the metropolitan church of St. Aaron ; the queen meanwhile being endued with similar state in St. Julius, the church of the Virgins. Afterwards the two royalties held their separate festivals in separate halls, as had been the custom in Troy, from which even more ancient and glorious city the Britons and Arthur, King of Britain, derive.

Caius, with a thousand young men in ermine, served the king's meat ; Bedver, with a similar number, his wine. The queen was similarly served. It is all a very high glory. The men are all celebrated for their valour, the women for their wit. Love encourages all to virtue, the women especially to chastity, the men especially to valour. But nobility in all things thrives in them all. The court of the great king is the centre and cynosure of the world.

What remains ? One other thing, and then the end. There come to the feast of Caerleon twelve ambassadors, wise old men, to demand from Arthur his submission to Rome. In the council that follows the king and his lords prepare to match themselves with Rome. Troy has been named, and in the scene that old war seems again to take on a new being—the descendants of Brutus against the descendants of Aeneas. Hoel, king of Armorien, declares that the Sibylline prophecies foretold that the Roman Empire should be held by three natives of Britain ; Brennus and Constantine are past, and now it is the turn of Arthur to hold the supreme dignity. Fate strengthens him. He appoints the queen and his nephew Modred to be his regents and prepares for war.

His opponent, Lucius Tiberius, procurator of Rome, gathers his own supporters. At a later moment he thinks of waiting for the aid of the Emperor Leo, but decides against it. But short of the imperial armies, the roll of Eastern kings reads like the list of the allies of Antony recorded in Virgil and in Shakespeare. Here are the kings of the Grecians and the Africans ; of Spain and Libya ; of Phrygia and Egypt, Babylon and Bithynia, Syria, Boeotia, and Crete ; of the Parthians and Medes. The invasion begins, and after Arthur has shown his personal valour by killing a giant at St. Michael's Mount, the armies engage under the golden dragon of Britain and the golden eagle of Rome. Many lords fall, including Caius and Bedver and Lucius Tiberius himself, whose body the victorious Arthur sends to the Senate with a message that this is the only tribute the Britons pay. He is about to cross the Alps for the final advance on Rome when news comes from Britain. The regents have violated their oaths. Modred has seized the crown, and the Queen Guenhumara has married him. Arthur returns, defeats Modred at the head of a mixed army of Britons, Saxons, Scots, Picts, Irish, and all malcontents, pursues him to Winchester, and there defeats him again. The queen, repenting, flees to Caerleon, and takes the vows among the nuns of St. Julius. Modred falls back into Cornwall and is there killed in the final battle. Arthur is mortally wounded, 'and being carried away to the isle of Avalon to be healed of his wounds, he gave up the crown of Britain to his kinsman Constantine, the son of Cador Duke of Cornwall, in the year of the Incarnation of our Lord five hundred and forty two '.

The Captain-General of the British kings, the leader of that cavalry force against the Saxons, had thus become quite another thing. He had been mythically raised into a grander throne than any of those old tribal chieftains, half his clients and half his patrons, had ever held. No doubt many elements had gone to the raising—all that Geoffrey had heard or read, all he knew of courts and cloisters, many fables and many facts. But unless there was once some intermediary tale which is now wholly lost (such as that book of the Archdeacon Walter Map to which he continually appeals, but in which no scholar now believes),[1] the new definition of Arthur was his alone. It was he, as things turned out, who determined what Arthur should be, and also what he should not be. He was to be a king and all but an emperor, but not a lover ; a commander, not a knight-errant ; central, not eccentric. His court and Table (but the Table has not yet come into being) were to accumulate to themselves all kinds of adventures, and finally the most terrible adventure of all, but there was then and has remained a curious respectability about it. It was (if you choose) a wish-fulfilment ; it was, as Geoffrey frankly stated, the kind of court over which every king wanted to preside and to which every lord wanted to belong.

[1] At this point I interrupted the reading to suggest that the view taken by A. Griscom (*The Historia Regum Britanniae of Geoffrey of Monmouth*, London, 1929) was different. The single word ' Griscom ' pencilled on the MS. doubtless means that Williams intended to give the matter further consideration.

He was the world's wonder, and it was proper that he should be, for he was entirely the kind of thing at which the world wanted to wonder—not perhaps in the five hundred and forty-second year of the Incarnation of our Lord, but certainly in the eleven hundred and thirty-ninth or thereabouts. The *Historia Regum*, as one might say, ' caught on '. Geoffrey had taken up a fable and so shaped and told it that it now had the potentiality of myth. Other and greater writers were to change it again into something more tremendous. But none of them should have written without, in the end, saying to their books, as the lord Galahad said to Bors of Lancelot : ' Salute me to my lord Geoffrey our father.'

And even the new figure of Arthur was not all. He gave us more—the name and supernatural strangeness of Merlin. It is true that in his account Merlin's chief activities are before Arthur's birth, and that he disappears from the tale at the point of the birth. He is there in relation to the king only to cause the magical substitution of Uther for Gorlois, and many other ways could have been found for the birth without that. But Geoffrey already had Merlin on his hands.

It seems likely that he invented him, as a person. Nennius had included a tale of a supernatural boy who had prophesied to Vortigern, the traitor British king who had called the Saxons over. Geoffrey took over and adapted this story. The name of Merlin may have come from the Celtic Myrddin. But Nennius knows nothing of Myrddin. He records that roughly at the time of Arthur, there were ' Talhiarn Cataguen and Neirin and Taliessin and Bluchbard and Cian, all famous at the same time in British poetry '. Myrddin was a bard, but not a prophet, let alone a wizard, in the Welsh tales. There is a poem called the *Dialogue of Myrddin and Taliessin*, a lament over a battle between two Northern chieftains, which ends

> Since I, Myrddin am next after Taliessin,
> Let my prediction become common.

' This is . . . the only thing in works not demonstrably

dependent on Geoffrey that suggests the possession of prophetic powers on the part of Merlin in all Welsh literature.' [1]

The supernatural boy of Nennius and the bard of Welsh poetry were now united by Geoffrey, who provided his combined figure with a birth of a new kind ; new, that is, as far as the story went, but not unrelated to other fables of the time. Vortigern was in danger from both Saxons and Britons and determined to build himself a new castle, but the earth always swallowed up the foundations. His wise men advised him that he must discover 'a lad who never had a father', and sprinkle his blood over mortar and stones before they would be firm. Outside Carmarthen the king's messengers heard a boy taunted by his companions with having had no father. They seized on the boy and his mother, who is found to be ' a daughter of the king of Demetio ', who lived in Carmarthen among the nuns of St. Peter. In Vortigern's presence the princess told her tale. She said : ' Lord, it is true I do not know who his father was. Once, when I and my companions were in our rooms, there appeared to me the shape of a handsome young man, who embraced and kissed me, and when he had been with me a little while, he suddenly vanished, and I never saw him again. But I often heard him speaking to me when I was alone, though I could never catch sight of him, and after he had haunted me in this way for a good time, I conceived and gave birth to this child. This, lord, is indeed what happened. No other could possibly be his father.' Vortigern again consulted one of his wise men who told him that other men had been conceived in this way. ' For,' he said, ' as Apuleius reports, in speaking of the god of Socrates, there are spirits between the earth and the moon whom we call daemons. Their nature is both angelic and human, and they are able whenever they choose to take on the shapes of men and have intercourse with women.'

In the later Middle Ages Geoffrey of Monmouth would not have been able to write so ; even in the next century it would have been dangerous. ' Those who dwell between the earth

[1] J. D. Bruce : *Evolution of Arthurian Romance.*

and the moon ' would have been too like ' those who come in the air ' at the trial of St. Joan of Arc : diabolic and dangerous to souls. But here they are not so. The thing changed, but at present there was a certain casualness even as regarded witchcraft and magic. It was, in general, believed to happen sometimes, and then it was thought to be a peculiar and rather horrid religious perversion. But it was also thought (very sensibly) that belief in it was almost as dangerous as the thing itself. And then there were, as one might say, a kind of select class of refined sorcerers attached to the households of great lords, together with alchemists, astrologers, clairvoyants, and so on, who were not unlike the college of two hundred philosophers in the City of Legions, the foundation of which might be suspected to have something to do with Merlin. Even as late as 1280 the Abbot of Whalley employed a clairvoyant to discover the body of his drowned brother ; it is true that, when this was discovered, he was excommunicated, but there the fact is. Merlin was something much greater than any such paid adept. He came from those other beings, faerie rather than diabolic, strange and comely, capable of high knowledge and sensuous delight.

It may perhaps be most convenient to pursue the subject of the birth and life of Merlin here. Geoffrey of Monmouth wrote a *Vita Merlini*, but in that the young wizard of the *Historia* has changed into a king and prophet of great age, the kind of figure with which the name of Merlin is more usually nowadays associated. He had not been so in the time of King Arthur, but this is long after the time of King Arthur. The king has been carried away in a boat by Taliessin who takes him ' to the island of apples which is called Fortunate ' ('Insula pomorum quae Fortunata vocatur '). Taliessin afterwards joins Merlin, and ' takes occasion to consider the various nature of the creation '. The poem becomes largely a dialogue *de natura rerum* by the two masters, interspersed with certain non-Arthurian adventures of Merlin.

But the next great development in the myth of Merlin came with Robert de Borron. It was perhaps here particularly affected by the general imagination of the time. Christendom, among its other formalizations of ideas, was formalizing the devil; that is, it was giving more and more attention to the devil. Neutral supernatural beings, ' between the cold moon and the earth ', half human, half angelic, were disappearing in favour of the wholly angelic, evil or good. It was impossible that a good angel should wish to have intercourse with women ; the text in Genesis about the sons of God seeing the daughters of men showed that. Any spirit who attempted it was bound to be evil. The next step was to say that evil spirits had attempted it. If so, they had failed. It was afterwards laid down by the authors of the *Malleus Maleficarum* that the devil cannot procreate by means of a woman, for he cannot produce human seed. But these refinements were not known to de Borron, or if so, he ignored them for the sake of his poem. He imagined a council held in hell after the Redemption, where, sitting ' in their own dimensions, like themselves ', the devils plotted to thwart it. They determined that the only method is to follow our Lord's method. There must be an incarnation ; flesh must be made amenable to their desires ; a pure maiden must conceive and bear a son. There, as so often, the conspirators of malice can only follow the conspiracy of divine largesse ; a true priest is necessary even for the Black Mass ; a clean maid is necessary even for the incarnation of the devil. One of the demonic powers agreed to make the attempt. He finds a girl who had made but a single slip ; once she forgot or neglected to say her prayers. The lightness (so to call it) of the fault marks her real spirituality ; grosser natures would not have served. Through that frailty he was enabled to approach her ; she miraculously conceived. When she knew it she went at once to a wise and holy man. By his interposition and the rites of the Church there was born at the proper time not Diabolus but Merlin. He inherited his spiritual father's knowledge and power, but without malice. It is this figure to which, as we shall see, de Borron attributes the union of the tale of the king with the tale of the Holy Grail.

It was this Merlin who later survived, though in modern times his connexion with the Grail has been lost. He has, in fact, been remembered only for two things : (i) for his wizardry, (ii) for his end. There was indeed an Elizabethan play, once attributed to William Shakespeare and William Rowley, and now only to Rowley, which is called *The Birth of Merlin*. It is a poor thing, with a good deal of the usual Elizabethan humour about the child's unknown father. His mother Joan is a peasant girl with no sign of spirituality about her ; and neither she nor anyone else talks the sure Shakespearean style. (Shakespeare himself alluded to Merlin twice : Hotspur is made to speak of him in reference to Glendower :

> I cannot choose ; sometimes he angers me
> With telling of the moldwarp and the ant,
> The dreamer Merlin and his prophecies.

And at the end of one of the heath scenes in *King Lear* the Fool, after seven couplets, concludes : ' This prophecy Merlin shall make ; for I live before his time.' Which, if we substituted some other name, is exactly such a prediction as Merlin himself might have made.)

Indeed the only English poets who have spoken almost worthily of that great master are Tennyson and Swinburne, and of the two Swinburne is for once the greater. It is he who carries on the strange birth, and he who even improved on the conclusion. Of the birth he says that Tristram, talking to Iseult on the deck of the ship bringing her to Cornwall, spoke of the king and the court, and of

> the might of Merlin's ancient mouth,
> The son of no man's loins, begot by doom
> In speechless sleep out of a spotless womb ;
> For sleeping among graves where none had rest
> And ominous houses of dead bones unblest
> Among the grey grass rough as old rent hair
> And wicked herbage whitening like despair
> And blown upon with blasts of dolorous breath
> From gaunt rare gaps and hollow doors of death,

A maid unspotted, senseless of the spell,
Felt not about her breathe some thing of hell
Whose child and hers was Merlin ; and to him
Great light from God gave sight of all things dim
And wisdom of all wondrous things, to say
What root should bear what fruit of night or day,
And sovereign speech and counsel higher than man ;
Wherefore his youth like age was wise and wan,
And his age sorrowful and fain to sleep ; . . .

His conclusion may be left for the present. In the old French romances the end of the grand adept was unworthy of him. I do not say that this was not deliberate ; I think it easily may have been, and meant to reduce the possessor of such supernatural wisdom to natural folly in the end. It is a tale told of all the great—of Solomon and Aristotle and Virgil—and whoever took it over for Merlin need not be supposed to be ignorant of what he was doing. The danger of an over-devotion to the study of sources is that we forget to attribute to those who used them a conscious intention in using them. Merlin is very old, and comes to dote on a girl named Viviane or Niniane. She was at first only twelve years of age ; as the centuries went by, she grew older and lost her character, till we are left with the greedy and shallow harlot of Tennyson. He tells her a spell which can hold even him enchanted and imprisoned. And one day, in that mysterious forest—Darnantes or Broceliande—she casts him into sleep and puts the spell in motion. He has had his reward from her—or perhaps he has not, for in some versions he only dreams that he has had her, and it is illusion, but he lies content. There is a gracious version in a fifteenth-century English prose version of de Borron ; which, after describing the enchantment, continues :

' And after that she went and sat down by him and laid his head in her lap and held him there till he did awake ; and then he looked round him, and him seemed he was in the fairest tower of the world, and the most strong, and found him laid in the fairest place that ever he lay before. And then he said to the damsel : " Lady, thou hast me deceived, but if ye will abide with me, for none but ye may undo this enchantment " ; and she said : " Fair sweet friend, I shall often times go out and ye shall have me in your arms, and I you ; and from thenceforth ye shall do all your pleasure." And she held him well covenant, for few hours there were of the night nor of the day, but she was with him. Nor ever after came Merlin out of that fortress that she had him in set ; but she went in and out when she would.'

II

GEOFFREY had written, in a general way, as if he were writing history ; that is, he had presented his book in the shape of an arranged and continuous record of past times. It was not the yearly annals of the chroniclers on the one hand, nor did it pretend to be romance on the other. His two most famous successors in the tale allowed themselves more freedom. One was [1] an Anglo-Norman clerk, born in Jersey, named Wace, who lived from about 1100 to about 1175, and about 1155 ' published ' his *Geste de Bretons* or (as others more usually called it) *Roman de Brut*. The prestige of the fabulous Trojan Brutus was still very strong ; the Britons were still derived from a city more ancient than Rome or Byzantium. Arthur, in his blood, drew from a deeper fount than any imperial house could ; one might even imagine that the final fall of his glory was not entirely without a dim relation to that other overthrow of Troy. Fifty or sixty years after his *Brut*, an English priest in Worcestershire produced another, which he frankly professed to found on Wace. Both were in verse ; the 15,000 lines of Wace become 30,000 in Layamon. But the style of the two poets was very different. Wace carried on the culture and medieval splendour of Geoffrey. Layamon wrote under the poetic influence of older poets, of the Anglo-Saxons. Wace is busy with courts and progresses ; Layamon with heroes and fighting. There is in Layamon something not unlike dialogue and exclamations ; where Wace gives silk and the polish of steel, Layamon gives cloth and the weight of steel. It is, however, not with their style but with their story that we are concerned.

[1] MS *They were.*

They both follow Geoffrey, but with added detail, the most important addition being the invention of the Round Table itself. The birth of Arthur is told by both in the same manner as in Geoffrey ; though in Layamon Merlin is introduced to Uther by means of a hermit. The hermit lived away to the west, in a wilderness, in a deep forest ; he had dwelled there many winters, and Merlin often came to him there. The hermit, coming back from Uther, saw Merlin standing under a tree and ran to him ; when they had embraced, Merlin (so wise as he was) spoke of the hermit's errand and forestalled him in revealing Uther's desire. He went on to prophesy of Arthur : ' All shall bow to him that dwells in Britain ; gleemen shall sing of him well ; noble poets shall eat of his breast ; men shall be drunk on his blood. . . . This word is secret ; neither Ygearne or Uther knows yet that such a son shall come from Uther Pendragon ; he is yet unbegot that shall govern all the people.'

Both the hermit and the forest are among the first—if they are not the very first—appearances in English, certainly in this myth, of those two images. Both, in various measure and in varied shapes, and under changing names, were to haunt the myth. The birth of Arthur was presently, by a dextrous twist, to be made canonical, or almost so, as near so as could be without involving Ygearne in a love too much like Guinevere's or Iseult's. Merlin was to know of even holier beings than hermits. And this western forest was to expand on all sides until presently it seemed as if Camelot and Caerleon and even Carbonek were but temporary clearings within it. But in Layamon Merlin goes on to Uther ; the transformations are accomplished and the child born. In Layamon also, and first, the elves take charge of him. ' They enchanted the babe with strong magic ; they gave him might to be the best of knights ; they gave him a second boon, to be a rich king ; they gave him a third, to live long ; they gave him good virtue, so that he was the most generous of living men. These things the elves gave ; well throve the child.' This again is one of the earliest relations of the king's person to faerie. He never came quite to belong to it ; he was always to be of this world, and it was fortunate, for that most serious of all quests in which his companionship, if not he, were to be involved, is not at all of faerie kind. Yet faerie hovered for centuries behind his shoulder, or indeed in his scabbard. Morgan le Fay was his sister, less explicable than that other sister who began as Anne and ended as Morgause, but was always the wife of King Lot and the mother of Mordred and Gawaine and the rest of the princes of the house of Orkney. At Badon, in both Wace and Layamon, the king wore a sword forged in Avalon, almost a faerie place—forged ' with magic craft', says Layamon, who calls it Caliburen, but Wace names it Excalibur. Layamon adds that his helmet was called Goswhit, and his shield Pridwen, on which was engraved in tracings of reddish gold, the image of the blessed and glorious Mary. Both poets add that the name of his spear was Ron.

It is Layamon who tells us of his cry when he is called to the throne by the bishops and lords : ' Lord Christ, God's Son, be to us now in aid that I may in life hold God's laws.' Both praise him with different phrases at this moment. Wace says that he was fifteen, tall and strong for his years, worthy of praise and glory ; haughty to the haughty, mild to the mild. He was one of Love's lovers ; he was above all other princes in courtesy and prowess, valour and largesse. Layamon adds that he was ' a father to the young, a comforter to the old, a judge to the foolish. He had no cook that was not a good champion, nor knight's servant that he was not good thane. The king held all his folk together with great bliss.'

There belonged, it may be held, to that bliss the most important new invention which these poets supplied—the making of the Round Table itself. The image may have come, and probably did come, from more ancient sources. Wace mentions its making, but only briefly : ' it was ordained that when this fair fellowship sat to meat, their chairs should be alike high, their service equal, none before or behind his companions ; and none could brag that he was exalted above any, for all alike were gathered round the board, and none was alien at the breaking of

Arthur's bread.' Layamon, however, gives a whole story. Arthur held Christmas court in London, during which jealousy and envy broke out in the household ; there were high words, blows, and eventually a great and bloody tumult, which the king himself in arms suppressed. He who began it was condemned to be thrown into a marsh ; his male kindred to be beheaded ; his nearest women folk to have their noses cut off. Anyone who in future causes a similar brawl is to be torn by wild horses ; so stern a judge to the foolish was the king. All the court swear on holy relics against any further outbreak. After this a man of Cornwall proposed that he should make for the king a great table, at which sixteen hundred men and more might be seated, within and without : ' there shall the high be equal with the low '. The king assented. The Table took four weeks to make, and when on the next day the court was assembled, ' all they one by one were seated, the high and the low '. ' It is not all sooth nor all falsehood that minstrels sing, ·but this is sooth of Arthur the king.'

Arthur's marriage takes place in both poems, though in Wace the queen is called Guinevere, in Layamon Wenhaver. In both she comes of Roman blood. Wace has the more princely description ; she is ' fair in face, courteous, delicate in person and motion, of a royal bearing, very sweet and of a ready tongue '. Arthur is said, in general, to love her wondrous well, but the single phrase has to serve. Even Wace, with his Love's lover, does not care to develop the theme, except that both he and Layamon follow Geoffrey in declaring that love encouraged chivalry and chastity. No knight could offer love to any lady till he had proved his worth ; then he might, ' and his friend was the more chaste as he was brave '. The phrase suggests —as we might from other sources suppose, and those not only Christian or doctrinal but imaginative and poetic—that chastity was more than a negation of lust ; it was a growing, heightening, and expanding thing. It was a state of spiritual being, and its spiritual expression was not at all inconsistent with marriage. It is to be remembered that chastity might be either married or virginal. Certainly the officials of the Church tended to stress the more austere type, but certainly also from the beginning there was a wider validity in the whole. But that lies more closely in Galahad and his companions on the quest.

It is against chastity and loyalty that the queen and Mordred offend. In both poems the queen's passion for Mordred is named. It is put forward as a fact and must be taken as a fact, for there has been no preparation. ' She had set her love,' says Wace, ' on her husband's sister's son.' ' The queen came to Mordred,' says Layamon, ' who was to her dearest of men.' Her end is alike in both : at York she hears of Mordred's defeat at Winchester ; she is highly troubled and full of remorse. ' Better were the dead than those who lived, in the eyes of Arthur's queen.' ' Woe was to her awhile that she was alive ! ' She escaped at night, accompanied by two lords, to the convent at Caerleon, where she had once been crowned. There she took the veil. ' Never again was fair lady heard or seen, never again found or known of men.' ' Nor for many years after did any man know if she were dead or if she were sunk in the water.'

As for the king, he was terribly wounded in the last battle, and had himself carried to Avalon to be healed of his wound. In both poems he commits the kingdom to the charge of Constantine, son of Cador Earl of Cornwall, to keep until he should come again. Layamon causes him to add that he will go to ' Argante the queen, fairest of maidens, an elf most fair ', who will make him whole with healing draughts. Wace gives the date—it was the year 642 of the Incarnation. Both say that Merlin prophesied the return. Wace holds that his words were doubtful, and that men have always doubted. ' Earl Constantine took the land into his charge and held it as he was bidden ; nevertheless, Arthur came not again.' But Layamon ended the tale on a higher note.

' Then was fulfilled what Merlin said once—that there should be much care of Arthur's departing. The Britons believe that he is alive, and dwells in Avalon with the fairest of all elves, and ever they expect when Arthur shall return. Never was any man born, of any lady chosen ever, who knew so much more of truth, to say more of Arthur. But of old while there was a wise man called Merlin ; he said with words—and sooth were the things he said—that an Arthur should yet come to help the English.'

CHAPTER IV

The Coming of Love

THE king had been established in his splendour. There was now another court, besides those of Alexander and Charlemagne, in which magnificence could exist, from which heroes could ride upon adventures, and to which their achievements could be returned. It was not yet certain that that potentiality would be accepted. The decision lay in the minds of poets and romancers, contemporary and future. The work of Geoffrey of Monmouth might have remained single and remote, and the work of Wace and Layamon might not seriously have complicated, though it might have heightened, the myth. The glory of the king would have remained a glory of wealth and war. That more than this happened was due primarily to the genius of two writers, Chrétien de Troyes and Robert de Borron. It was their choice of—say, their allegiance to—the king which determined the future.

They belonged, both of them, to that Anglo-French civilization which now ruled in the West. The name of one of its own princes is indirectly connected with Arthur—the name of Henry II Plantagenet, King of England and Duke of Normandy, Anjou, and (by his wife Eleanor) of Acquitaine. It was in his reign that the Abbot of the Benedictine monastery at Glastonbury, Henry of Blois, determined to have excavations made. Glastonbury had been identified with Avalon ; also, it was the place where Joseph of Arimathea had set the Grail. Discovery was said to confirm at least the first myth, the myth of royalty. At a depth of sixteen feet, a coffin of oak was found, on which was an inscription : ' Hic jacet sepultus inclitus rex Arthurus in insula Avalonis.' Within it were bones and (it is said) golden hair which when a monk lifted it fell into nothing.

In France there was a development in letters, also indirectly relating the Pendragon to the Plantagenet. The earliest name is that of a certain Marie de France who is generally identified with Marie, Countess of Champagne. It is to be hoped that the identification may be correct, for Marie would then indeed be not only a daughter of France, since the Countess of Champagne was the daughter of Louis VII, but step-sister-in-law to England, through Eleanor the wife of the Plantagenet. Marie de France wrote certain *lais* which she dedicated to King Henry, in one of which, though only in one, the court of Arthur is invoked. Lanval, in the *lai* of that name, is one of his knights, and is loved by his queen. From the beginning of the Matter of Britain, the queen seems to have been, as it were, doomed to infidelity. Her husband was not to love, in that kind, at all, and she was to love too much. In a literary sense, indeed, the later Lancelot was to be her salvation, for it was he by whom she was to endure a great passion and to come to some penitence, whereas otherwise she might have remained linked with a score of unknown names. It may be that she was taught to love so because those who wrote of her would not have the queen of Arthur less than Iseult the queen of Mark, whose passion for Tristan was already a theme of song. But in *Lanval* she loves without return, for the knight himself has a fairy mistress who carries him off— where but to Avalon, which is her own land and ' a very fair island ' ?

But if Marie of France was also Marie of Champagne, she had a client who did more for King Arthur than she. The Countess held her court at Troyes and made it a centre of this new and metaphysical civilization, and even more a centre of one of the lesser cults which were thriving in it. There was a kind of cult of sorcery, but this the Countess does not seem to have encouraged, any more than (for all that one can see) she encouraged that other cult of sanctity. What she did encourage was the art of poetry and the cult of courtly love. Among the poets who surrounded her was a certain Chrétien, called from his place of lodging de Troyes. He was there from 1160 to 1172 ; he is said to have been a herald and to have visited England—

both of which are pleasant notions and quite credible. But we do not know. By 1160 the *Historia* of Geoffrey of Monmouth had been 'out' some twenty years. Chrétien (as he himself tells us) had translated Ovid and written a poem on Tristan ; neither of these remain. An earlier poem on Tristan had been written by a certain Beroul, but in this there was no allusion to Arthur. Here again the beginning points the way ; Tristan, even in Malory, has never sat quite willingly at the Table. He is splendid and noble, but something always of an outland man. At Troyes Chrétien produced four poems—*Erec et Enide, Cligès, Lancelot, Yvain* ; it is thought, in that order. He was presently at another court to produce another poem, *Perlesvaux*. All these poems take advantage of the superb background which had been provided. It was there for the using, and Chrétien chose to use it, and to do almost as much for it as his predecessor Geoffrey and his successor Robert. This applies especially to the *Lancelot*. But all four eulogize the great king. The *Erec* begins : ' In spring, at Easter, King Arthur held court at Cardigan ', and proceeds with an adventure on which the king himself rides, the hunt of the White Hart. The *Cligès* says (after a paragraph or so) : ' Alexander (the son of the Emperor at Byzantium—even he) had heard of King Arthur, who was reigning then, and of the chivalry who were about him, through whom he was honoured and feared in all parts of the world.' The *Lancelot* begins : ' On a certain day of the Ascension King Arthur had come from Caerleon and held a magnificent court at Camelot ' ; and the *Yvain* : ' That good King Arthur of Britain, from whom all of us learn constancy and courage, held once, upon that precious feast which is called Pentecost, a rich and royal court at Cardoal in Wales.' *Erec* contains a list of some of the lords. ' Gawaine should be named first of all that excelling chivalry ; next was Erec, the son of Lac ; and third, Lancelot of the Lake. Gornemant of Gohort was fourth ; the Handsome Coward fifth. The sixth was the Ugly Brave, the seventh Maliant of Liz, the eighth Marduit the Wise, the ninth Didinel the Wild ; and let Gardelen be called the tenth, for he was a goodly man.

I will name the rest as the names may come, for the numbers inconvenience me.' Some names among 'the rest' are of interest. Tristan was there, who never laughed ; he sat beside Bliobleheris ; Girflet the son of Do, who in the later Malory has become the rather shattering (because unexplained) Giroflet fils de Dieu ; Loholt, ' the son of King Arthur, a youth of great merit', and Gronosis, ' versed in evil', the son of Kay the Seneschal—both these were to disappear entirely ; King Lot, of whom no more is said. Besides these companions of the royal chivalry—the Round Table, of course, had not yet been invented —there were the dukes and kings whom King Arthur summoned to his court. There was Maheloas, ' a great baron, lord of the isle of Voirre, where no thunder is heard and no lightning strikes ; there are no storms ; no toads or serpents dwell in it ; and it is never either too hot or too cold.' This sounds like the island of Avalon, but it is not, for the lord of Avalon was there too, Guigomar, a friend of Morgan the Fay. King Ban of Gornoret brought two hundred beardless young men, all carrying hawks ; and King Kerrin of Riel three hundred white-bearded sages, of whom the youngest is sevenscore years old. There also was the King of the Antipodes, the smallest of all dwarfs. It is, here, a court almost as strange as that other which surrounded Solomon, son of David, king in Jerusalem, where angels and Afrits, and all the quarters of the world, came ; though the Ring on his finger exercised a power over them which no property of King Arthur's ever had.

It will have been noticed that the first of the knights named is Gawaine, and this holds everywhere in Chrétien. Gawaine is the king's nephew, and is always treated as being next to the king. ' Welcome,' says a lady in *Yvain*, receiving the court, ' welcome a hundred thousand times to my lord the king, and blessed be his nephew, my lord Gawaine.' He is the most notable of all, and the only one who is permanently equal to the various different heroes of the poems. Lancelot, outside the poem named after him, is only mentioned twice ; once in *Erec*, as above ; and the second time in *Cligès*, where it is admitted that he does not lack courage but it is also said that if Cligès were dressed in a sack and Lancelot in silver and gold, Cligès would be the fairer. Lancelot is overthrown ; ' he could not help himself ; he gave himself up to Cligès '. But Cligès, of course, could not overcome Gawaine ; they fought equally, and the king had to make peace between them. Even in the *Lancelot* itself, Gawaine is ' the most admired and most famous knight upon whom ever the sign of the Cross was made '. He is the noble friend and champion of lesser knights. He is, in fact, exactly what the chief knight should be and what Lancelot was afterwards to become ; and one might think that Lancelot's first step towards it was when it was said of him, in his own particular poem, that ' Gawaine would not have cared to be king, if he could not have had Lancelot by his side '.

All these lords, if not first named in Chrétien, are first grouped and distinguished by him. But the real new power whom he brought into that assembly, the lord who up to now had hardly been named there, and had had no chance to be superbly tyrannical over the chivalry, was Love itself. Geoffrey of Monmouth had spoken of it. But now Love was to be the master as much as the king and Love the theme as much as war. It was, of course, a particular kind of Love ; Love as it appeared in that age and to the court of Troyes, enlivened by Chrétien's genius. It was ' courtly love '. On the other hand the reader who before looking at Chrétien has heard a good deal of this, its manners, its moralities and immoralities, its literature and its effects, may at first when he does look at Chrétien be a little surprised to find that it is not only real and recognizable but even respectable. The *Lancelot* may, for the moment, be excepted from this generalization. But the *Erec* depends upon a married relationship ; the whole question is of the effect of a state of settled love upon a man's proper activities. And in the *Cligès* marriage is twice stressed : the first time, by a general statement ; the second, by the details of the story.

In both poems the lovers examine themselves, in the literary manner of the day, upon this astonishing passion. They dilate on the effect that this Grand Master of body and mind has on them. They do not very much go into the soul ; there is nothing of Dante here, and nothing of what, after Dante had finished with it, has been meant by romantic love. This is the early style, and not yet mature. Soredamours, who is in love with Alexander, speaks to herself of her love :

'Shall I call him by his name or shall I call him friend ? Friend ? Not I ; but what then ? the name of friend is fair and sweet to speak. . . . He would not lie if he were to call me his sweet friend. And should I if I spoke so to him ? . . . If I spoke his name, I should be afraid of stumbling in the middle ; but " friend "—I could soon speak that short word. I would be willing to shed my blood if his name were simply " my sweet friend ".'

It is Guinevere who brings the lovers together. She causes them to be called to her and addresses them.

'Alexander, love is worse than hate when it torments its devotees. Lovers do not know what they are doing when they hide from each other their passion. Love is a serious business, and whoever is not bold enough to lay the foundation properly will never be able to finish the building. Both of you are acting foolishly in maintaining this silence ; concealment will kill you, and then you will have murdered Love. Now my counsel to you is to put no tyranny and to seek no temporary delight in Love, but to be joined together in all honour in marriage ; thus Love will, I believe, endure a great while. Do but agree, and I will take it on myself to arrange the marriage.'

Alexander answers that, if he had dared, he would have spoken long ago ; silence has indeed been hard. 'But it may be that this maid does not choose to be mine or that I should be hers. Even then, though she does not give me the right, I will put myself in her hands.' Soredamours answers falteringly that she is—all of her, will, heart, and body—at the disposal of the queen. Guinevere laughs, embraces them, and says : 'I give each one of you to the other. Take, Soredamours, what is yours, and you, Alexander, what is yours.'

The queen here is something nobler than the barely visible

Guanhumara and than she who loved Lanval. There is in her
a touch of the Guinevere she was to become, she who in Malory
said to the court, at the first appearance of Galahad : ' I may well
suppose that Sir Lancelot begat him on King Pelles' daughter,
by the which he was made to lie, by enchantment, and his name
is Galahad. I would fain see him, said the queen, for he must
needs be a noble man, for so is his father that him begat ; I report
me unto all the Table Round.' It is true she was there speaking
outside marriage, and yet perhaps not, for it would be improper
to assume that the queen was not as much in love with the
nobility of Lancelot as with his person ; and if his person sometimes dominated his nobility in her, the realism is truer so. But
the development of that royal figure must be left till a later
chapter. But the main point is her reference to marriage ; it
is thus that Love is to be built and thus that it is to endure.
Whatever other poets did, whatever in another poem Chrétien
himself did, here the paramount opportunity and privilege of
marriage is laid down. In the second part of the poem, which
deals with the adventures of Alexander's son Cligès, marriage
is safeguarded by the details. Alexander's brother Alis has
seized the imperial throne. Alexander consents to leave him in
peace, provided he swears not to marry, which he does. But
after Alexander's death, he breaks his oath and proceeds to espouse
and to marry Fénice, the daughter of the Emperor of the West.
The marriage is thus null and void from the beginning. Fénice
is, of course, in love with Cligès, and he with her. But they
conceal it, ' There was no eye so keen nor ear so sharp as to
gather from anything seen or heard that there was love between
those two.' Cligès leaves for Britain and King Arthur ; Fénice
for Byzantium. There her nurse makes a drink for the Emperor
by which he falls into illusion, and dreams that he has his pleasure
with Fénice, while she lies safe by his side, ' as if there were a wall
between them '. It is a magical preservation of her virginity,
but it is meant to be justified by the Emperor's perjury. Cligès
returns and entreats Fénice to escape with him. But she will not
do it so. ' Everyone,' she says, ' when we had gone, would

speak evil of our love ; they would not believe the truth ;
indeed, they could not. They would talk of us as if we were
Tristan and Iseult the Fair.' It has been said of this that she is
merely being anxious about her reputation, but this is hardly
fair. She quotes St. Paul ; she is anxious not to give scandal.
Our own age has largely lost that fear, perhaps because we are
sensitive to the other danger of hypocrisy, so that we have come
to think that sin loses half its evil by losing all its secrecy, unless
for personal reasons of kindness. But this is hardly so ; and
scandal, it seems, was to Chrétien a very real harm. If she could
be thought dead . . . and by the help of another potion she
arranges to be thought dead, in spite of incredible tortures by
rods and by melted lead applied by the doctors. She suffers all
this—for her reputation ? say rather, for her love and for what
she thought the common good. An empress, even an un-
canonical empress, must not be generally thought to have run
off with her lover. Eventually her device succeeds, though she
is afterwards discovered and compelled after all to escape with
Cligès to King Arthur. Cligès makes ' claim and protest to the
king that his uncle the emperor had disloyally taken a wife,
when he had sworn he would never marry all his life. And the
king answered that he would gather a thousand ships and fill
them with knights, and three thousand with men-at-arms, so
that no city or borough, town or castle, could resist him, and
with this fleet he will set out for Byzantium'. This is the
judgement of Arthur, the master of courtesy and chivalry. But
news comes that the emperor is dead, and the lovers return to
reign. ' And Cligès still called his wife mistress and love, and
she had no loss of love to complain of, for he loved her always
as his lady, and she him as her lover, and every day their love
grew stronger.' Which was what the queen Guinevere had
promised his father.

It is true that in the *Lancelot* there is a difference. This is a
story of an abduction of Guinevere. Sir Edmund Chambers has
said that ' as the schoolgirl wrote, she was a lady very much
subject to the misfortune of being run away with '. It might be

urged on her behalf that the poets and romancers could think of very little else for her to do or be. They had refused her a family. Loholt, the son of Arthur, made an appearance in *Erec*, but he was killed off in Chrétien's own later poem, *Perlesvaux*, and I doubt if (since then) anyone except Sir Walter Scott has been daring enough to imagine an heir to Arthur. Wace indeed had lamented that he was ' a childless man ', with ' the sorer sorrow '. Her lovers were always leaving her, to ride out on quests, ' for fear of their reputation '. The king, except here and there, is never shown to have any great interest in her nor she in him, though they appear together superbly in public. Until the tragic shock of the close was invented, she was not allowed to have a concern for religion, nor (more oddly, perhaps, considering everything) was she allowed to form such a court of love and poetry as seems to have existed at Troyes. No ; she had little to do but to be abducted and to be rescued, until her poets filled her empty life with Lancelot.

But in the poem of that name she is not yet fully herself. She is carried away by Meleagaunt to the country of his father King Bagdemagus. This country is clearly derived from one of those lands of the dead made familiar in more ancient tales. But in the poem of Troyes it is not allowed to have its terrifying identity ; only in glimpses can we catch sight of its original nature, through the ordered process of the love-tale. In the hither province of Bagdemagus's country are many of the people of the land of Logres who are held captive there ' by the custom of the land '. ' No stranger enters this land but he is compelled to stay.' He is not imprisoned in the ordinary sense ; he may be free and rich. But he can never again cross the frontier back to Logres. After this, something more than mere adventure seems to hide in the account of the two bridges ; the one under water, and as much water above as below ; the other, the edge of a sharp sword, as long as two lances. It is here that the name of Logres seems to be first used for King Arthur's land ; its derivation is said to be from the Welsh Lloegr, a land of faerie which was also Britain or within Britain. But none of these things are developed by Chrétien ; they only strike the reader suddenly with something more like a faint terror than the other tales of the king have anywhere suggested. Mr. C. S. Lewis has said that ' it is one of Chrétien's misfortunes that the dark and tremendous suggestions of the Celtic myth that lurk in the background of his story should so far (for a modern reader) overshadow the love and adventure of the foreground '. But then the Middle Ages were, to themselves, modern.

It was to the foreground that Chrétien attended, and the foreground in the *Lancelot* (much more than in the other poems) was courtly love, love as it was talked and sung and even practised in courts. Courts in that century had, like so many things, a freedom they had not long possessed ; there was room and time to be refined, and codes by which to be refined. In Provence they had refined love into a code, and through Europe the men and women of the courts copied Provence. It may, however, be added that in some respects at least Provence had first copied life. Some of our modern discussions on courtly love seem to begin by removing it wholly from human experience. It was, no doubt, a separation and an exaggeration of what was at best only one element in human experience, and at its worst it became, no doubt, as all such separations and exaggerations will, a false caricature of even that element. People in whom it hardly existed at all had to pretend not only that it existed, but that practically nothing else existed. Something of the same overstrained effort was true of Geneva under Calvin and is all but true of England under democracy. But that does not alter the fact that the democratic effort is part of the English experience, that the Will of God was a very serious part of the experience of many holy souls in Geneva, and that the code of courtly love expressed a particular kind of passion felt by many lovers then and now. Thus the *Lancelot* said of its hero that he knelt to the queen, ' for in no holy body had he such belief '. The physical beauty of Guinevere appeared to him a thing literally transcendental. This is, no doubt, what the code told him he ought to feel and in any case how he ought to behave. It will not do, however, to forget that a great number of lovers have felt like this. To codify—almost to institutionalize—is perhaps unwise, but the folly (if it is a folly) does not abolish the original reality ; any more than the imbecilities of some of the disciples of Wordsworth about flowers and mountains alter the fact that Wordsworth and many others have been moved and exalted by flowers and mountains. The body of the beloved appears vital with holiness ; the physical flesh is glorious with sanctity—not her sanctity, but its own. It is gay and natural to genuflect to it. Such an experience may exist before marriage, in marriage, and after marriage ; it is the *stupor* of which Dante wrote and which we, when we read of it, immediately recognize. The code was, no doubt, an invention, but not the passion that caused the code. That it sometimes led—and leads—to adultery no more disproves its validity than the fact that it may lead to marriage or renunciation proves it. It may be a temptation, exactly as Isabella in *Measure for Measure* was a temptation to Angelo. But it would seem difficult to deny the apparent enskying and sainting of Isabella merely because Angelo was tempted by it.

But at this time the whole of this particular experience was separated, arranged, codified, and to a large extent falsified in the process. It was also made fashionable and falsified still further. In Chrétien's *Lancelot* one can almost see the thing happening. Geoffrey of Monmouth had alluded to that love in the king's court which encouraged all lovers to virtue, but he had not gone into the matter. Wace had said that the king and his knighthood were Love's lovers, but he too had contented himself with the suggestion of a general glow of bright affection. It is a part of the whole glory ; it is neither made very particular in itself, nor is it particularized in any of the personages. It is more in the nature of the masculine companionship than markedly between men and women ; that, at least, is the kind of love that dominates. The king, when he hears of the death of Gawaine, is said to feel a special grief : ' there too was Gawaine his nephew killed ; and Arthur made great sorrow over him ; for this knight was dearer to him than any other man '. But the only peer of Arthur, so far, who is allowed to have any love-interest is Mordred, and it is in general rather the queen, the king's wife, rather than the woman, his own lady, whom he seizes and marries. The deed is political rather than amorous. Love, however, was now to enter the court, and Love was to be, then and there, courtly love. Lancelot was, apparently by Chrétien's choice or by that of his patron, the Countess of Champagne, to be presented in that kind as the proper and perfect lover. But his refined perfection is not wholly alien.

The most famous incident of his career, after that manner and in this poem, is that of the cart; from which afterwards a prose version of the poem derived its name, *La Conte de la Charette*. It comes close to the original abduction of the queen. Lancelot followed, and after him Gawaine. Lancelot lost his horse, apparently in a battle with Meleagaunt, and presently overtook a cart driven by a dwarf. Now at that time a cart was a rare thing, and evil. There was only one in each town, and it was used to expose and carry to execution, thieves, murderers, traitors, and other criminals. Anyone who had been carried in a cart lost all reputation and legal right; he was dead in law, and could no more show himself in courts or towns. Anyone who met a cart crossed himself and said a prayer. It is possible that this is not without some relation to the queen being carried to the kingdom of the dead; at least, that relation obviously proposes itself to us, though Chrétien has not much use for it. Lancelot asked the dwarf for news of the queen; the dwarf answered that if the knight would mount the cart, he should presently hear of her. For a couple of steps Lancelot hesitated. Reason and Love dispute, for that time, within him. Reason loses; Love triumphs; he climbs in. Presently, when he had undergone many adventures, and crossed the sword-bridge, and overcome Meleagaunt, he was brought by Bagdemagus to the queen, whom he had now liberated. But she had heard of his hesitation. She threw him a cold look and would not speak to him. Lancelot, ' feeling very helpless ' (how one's heart leaps at that phrase ! how one recognizes the chilly glance, the silent mouth !), decided that his fault must be in having ridden in the cart at all. This, of course, is exactly what a man would think, and might even sometimes be quite right in thinking ; one never quite knows which way the admirable feminine mind will spring. He was wrong ; his fault lay only in his delay. Presently, after an alarm of death on both sides, she softened. He dared to ask how he had offended her. She answered : ' You must remember that you were not at all in a hurry to get in that cart ; you went two good steps before you did.' Lancelot abased himself profoundly. ' For God's sake, lady, take my amends, and tell me if you can forgive me.' The queen said : ' Willingly ; I forgive you entirely.'

No doubt this is an extreme example of courtly love. But no doubt also it is based on general human experience. The delay in action may, to a woman, mean more than the action itself. ' I'm not convinced by proofs but signs ' says Patmore's young woman ; and all masculine heroism without feminine tact is apt to go wrong. Where one expected gratitude (not that Lancelot did) one finds austerity. Oh perhaps the Provençals manipulated love too much, but undoubtedly they knew what they were manipulating !

Lancelot ' loved more than Pyramus, if that were possible '. On one occasion he and ' a damsel ' found near a spring a comb of gilded ivory in which golden hairs were tangled. The girl said she was sure it belonged to the queen. ' " There are many kings and queens ; which do you mean ? " " Fair lord, I speak of King Arthur's wife." ' Lancelot, at the sudden sentence, all but fainted (a Provençal lover ; but it happens outside Provence ; he is not perhaps so fortunate who has never felt his colour change at such an unexpected pang). He keeps the hair—' he despises essence of pearl, treacle, and the cure for pleurisy ; he does not need St. Martin or St. James ; he puts such great trust in this hair.' So the handkerchief of the beloved in its degree is sometimes much like the Veronican ; the face of Love is there.

On the other hand when, at a tournament, Lancelot on the

first day triumphed, and the queen on the second sent him word he was to do his worst, he obeyed, for he did not mind being thought cowardly, so only that he did his lady's will—it is then almost impossible not to feel that the convention is being pressed beyond likelihood ; or if it is not, that the likelihood of that age is indeed different from ours. A woman—even a queen—ought not so to interfere in a man's business. It may be that one ought to stop fighting—or writing a poem or doing excavations—if one's lady wishes, but that she should bid one fight badly or write a poor poem or do silly excavations : this even Love can hardly command. Reason has a word to say. Alas, if Reason had, in that day Reason lost. It is not the smallest advantage of the divine Dante a century and a half later that he believed Love to aid Reason ' in all things proper to Reason '. But then the image of Beatrice was ' of so noble a virtue ' that it is impossible to imagine her commanding her lover to write a bad poem for her sole whim. There is something about Guinevere—even Malory's Guinevere—which does not make it quite impossible for her. It is a little perhaps because, until the end, she is never shown to us in a moral distress over her marriage and her love. She might have been sinful, but she should have been troubled ; not being, she remains faintly more egotistic than high literature allows.

In the *Lancelot* there is no doubt about the love affair. When they were reconciled Lancelot came to the queen by night. In order to enter her room he had to bend and wrench out the bars of the window and in doing so he cut his fingers. He did not notice it, so intent was he on the queen. In the morning ' his body goes and his heart stays ; yet his body so far stays that the blood which has fallen from his fingers stains the queen's bed '. He straightened the bars behind him ; then he bowed towards the room as if towards a shrine. The two elements of a proper worship and (*pace* the adultery) a proper sensuality are too close together for our taste. The maxim for any love affair is ' Play and pray ; but on the whole do not pray when you are playing and do not play when you are praying.' We cannot yet manage such simultaneities, and it is difficult for us to believe that the early Middle Ages could. A formal genuflection may be all that is meant, but even that—then and there—is distasteful.

However this may be, the *Lancelot* is the first statement of the love between Lancelot and the queen. It is also, so to speak, the promotion of Lancelot. Gawaine, who had followed him, but had not been much use, rebuked those at Arthur's court who praised him. ' " These honours are shameful to me, for I did not reach the queen in time to free her. But Lancelot was there in time and won such honour as was never won by any other knight." ' This, as one might say, settled the matter not only in the poem, but outside the poem. If the queen was to be loved and rescued it was Lancelot who was to do it. If Lancelot was to do it, and to be the queen's lover, he was to become more and more important. Subject to the genius of future poets, he must become in fact the rival—in some sense, the equal—of the king. To make a proper relationahip, he and the king must each in turn outgrow the other. At the moment when Lancelot bent and pulled the bars of the window of the queen's room, it was determined that, for all the courtly conventions in which it was begun, it was to be a business of sensuality as well as of adoration. Unless any greater genius interfered with that development, the sensual passion would be likely to grow. No greater genius did. ' So fair, so bold, so serene ', the king Bagdemagus called Lancelot ; these qualities, but shaken, troubled, and darkened by that unhappy and indulged passion were to be with him to the end. Love had indeed come to the court of Arthur, and presently a ruin beyond the dreams of courtly love was to follow it.

CHAPTER V

The Coming of the Grail

THE last poem written by Chrétien de Troyes is the first European poem in which an object called ' a grail ' certainly appears. The poem was in fact originally called *Le Conte du Graal* ; afterwards it became known as *Perceval*. It was written, Chrétien says, at the suggestion of Philip, Count of Flanders, to whose court the poet had apparently transferred himself, and ' from a book which the Count gave me '. The Count is known to have left Flanders for the Holy Land in 1190 and died there in 1191. Chrétien is thought to have been engaged on the poem a little earlier, between 1174 and 1180, and to have died before he had finished it. It was then taken up by other writers, and Chrétien's original 10,000 lines were expanded to over 60,000. In these continuations the original grail underwent development ; it became particular and the grand material object of Christian myth.

A second group of poems—meant as one—took up the subject. They were written by Robert de Borron. There were three of these poems, of which two remain : *Joseph d'Arimathie, Merlin*, and a *Perceval* known to us only in a later prose version. De Borron was a client of Gautier de Montbeliard, at whose request the poem was composed. Gautier too left France ; in 1199 he was in Italy ; in 1201 in Palestine. There he became Constable of Jerusalem. It will be remembered that the Pope Urban II had proclaimed the First Crusade in 1095 and that from then onwards for a couple of centuries the thought of the liberation of the Holy Places occupied a definite place in the imagination of Western Europe. The word ' liberation ' is useful here, because we have ourselves known it. It was no more the only cause of the Crusades than the liberation of Europe was the only cause of our own war. Self-preservation—physical and economical—from that threatening mass of Islam came in—as a similar preservation did with us. But as that other thought moved seriously and widely among us, so with them. It would be as false to say that they did not think of Jerusalem as that we did not think of Paris. Jerusalem was recovered for the West (to which it was always considered to belong) in 1099. In 1187 it was again captured by Saladin. The three chief lords of the West—Philip Augustus King of France, Richard Plantagenet King of England, Frederick Barbarossa the Emperor in the West —moved to free it. It was under the continuous impulse of this desire for liberation that the Count of Flanders and the lord of Montbeliard moved—the latter certainly in connexion with that spectacular Third Crusade. It is true it failed ; the title of Constable of Jerusalem was a vain brag or a deliberate challenge. But it was not known that it would fail.

There were, therefore, in that twelfth century, two influences of this realistic kind on Chrétien and de Borron. The first was the conversation, referred to in the first chapter, on the Blessed Sacrament which was conducted among the intellectuals, among the semi-intellectuals, and among the pseudo-intellectuals. It was not, of course, supposed to be a conversation on an unimportant point of theology ; it was a discussion on something that was going on in every parish in Europe. The second influence was the general idea of the crusades for the Holy Places. Abandon the disputes and the wars, and it still remains true that the thought of the Eucharist and the thought of Jerusalem were in the minds of most men. They were, then, the modern subjects, and the poets and romancers treated them in their own modern way. Chrétien declares that his story is ' the best tale that has ever been told in royal courts '. De Borron says that until he wrote ' the great history of the Holy Grail had never been treated by mortal man '.

This sense of a living, exciting, and topical subject is still prominent in the early part of the next century, which was the period of the great prose romances. These were partly prose versions of the poems and partly new compositions. There were brought to bear on the subject a number of fresh romantic intelligences, whose names are unknown to us. They altered ; they enlarged ; they invented. They saw the opportunities their predecessors had missed ; and peculiarly they saw one opportunity—they devised a mythically satisfying Achievement of the Grail ; and eventually they brought the whole together in one great work, consisting (as one may say) of five parts—*L'Estoire du Saint Graal, L'Estoire de Merlin, L'Estoire de Lancelot, La Queste del Saint Graal,* and *Le Mort d'Artu.* This great achievement—in a literary sense—of the Grail is held to have been mainly concluded by 1230. And the important thing about it is that it was a literary achievement. It is occasionally forgotten, or seems to be, in the great scholarly discussions, that anyone who is writing a poem or a romance is primarily writing a poem or a romance. He will, of course, be affected, as the Crusaders in their task were affected, by all sorts of other things—his religious views, his political views, his need of money, the necessity for haste, the instructions of a patron, carelessness, forgetfulness, foolishness. But he is primarily concerned with making a satisfactory book. He may borrow anything from anywhere—if he thinks it makes a better book. He may leave out anything from anywhere—if he thinks it makes a better book. And this (it can hardly be doubted), rather than anything else, was the first cause of the invention of the glorious and sacred figure of Galahad.

It is impossible, and (were it possible) undesirable, in this volume to go in any but the briefest way into the many variations of the myth which lie between the *Conte du Graal* and the *Queste del Saint Graal,* or into the complex questions of date, origin, and relationship. They all lie behind Malory, and it is Malory's book which is for English readers the record book of Arthur and of the Grail. It is, however, permissible to note a few of the points of development. We may say that there were [five] [1] of them :

(i) The determination of the Grail as a subject, and the invention of its history.

[1] I have supplied this word : the MS. has a blank space. [C. S. L.]

(ii) The relation of this—at first generally ; then definitely through Merlin—with the figure of King Arthur.

(iii) The invention of the Dolorous Blow.

(iv) The development of the love of Lancelot and Guinevere.

(v) The invention of Galahad.

(i) Chrétien's *Conte du Graal* dealt with the adventure of a youth named Perceval, afterwards Perceval le Gallois, or Perceval of Wales. He was the son of a widow who wished to keep him with her at home. But he met by chance certain knights of King Arthur's court, whom he questioned. Excited by this, he determined to go to the court and there achieve knighthood. He set out ; as he went, he looked back and saw his mother fall to the ground, fainting with grief. He would not return ; he went on, and came to the court where (after the usual difficult episode with Sir Kay, who was becoming the most churlish of all the lords) he went off in pursuit of a Red Knight, by killing whom he supplied himself with armour. He then remained for some time with an old knight, Gournemant, who taught him the usage of chivalry and eventually knighted him, giving him three pieces of advice—to be slow to speak, to be slow to ask questions, and to be slow to quote his mother's sayings on all occasions. He then came to the town and castle of Beaurepair where Gournemant's niece Blanchfleur lived. She was threatened by an evil king and asked Perceval's help. After the two young people had spent the night together, Perceval overthrew the king, sent him to Arthur, and presently departed. He came to a river where two men were fishing from a boat. One of them directed him to a castle close by. There Perceval was taken into the hall, where were four hundred men sitting round a fire, and an old man lying on a couch. The old man gave him a sword on which was an inscription that it will break only in one peril, and that known only to the maker. Presently a squire entered, bearing a lance from the point of which a drop of blood continually ran down ; then came two more squires, each carrying a ten-branched candlestick ; and after them a damsel bearing ' a grail '. What the grail was is not defined ; only it is said that the light which shone from it wholly abolished the blaze of the candles which preceded it. After it came another damsel carrying a silver plate. The pageant passed between the couch and the fire and went out. Perceval, remembering Gournemant's advice, did not venture to ask any question. Supper was served in the hall, and with each course the grail was brought in and carried to an inner room where some unknown person was fed with a Host from it. Perceval still asked nothing. He was taken to his chamber ; the next morning he found the castle deserted and his horse waiting, ready saddled, outside it. Riding away, he presently came to a place where a knight was lying dead and a girl weeping over him. It was from her that he now learnt that the Fisherman and the old man of the castle were the same person—a king who had been mysteriously wounded by a spear through the thigh. If only (she went on) Perceval had asked what was the meaning of the pageant he had seen, the king would have been healed and the land should have had great good. She also told him that his mother was dead, and that he was responsible, for she had died from sorrow at his departure. Later in the poem this is confirmed by a hermit who is Perceval's uncle and adds that Perceval is in a state of sin because of his mother's death ; it is this sin which prevented him asking the question. After this the poem involved itself— as far as Chrétien went—with adventures of Perceval, Gawaine, and others which have no immediately significant connexion with the Grail.

Here then are the earlier images—the strange castle, the wounded king, the sword, the bleeding lance, the grail, the mysterious nourishment, the unasked question, and the consequent lack of some great good. There is, in the unfinished poem, no attempt at explanation. But there are three critical comments to be made. The first is simply that the wound in the thighs is primarily a wound in the thighs. It is, no doubt, being in the thighs, symbolical of sex or fertility or anything else of that sort. But at least it is a wound which has got to be somehow explained.

The explanation, if we had had it, might have been as unsatisfactory as many of the explanations in the Elizabethan drama. But the story, unless it were to drop the Wounded King altogether, had got to deal with it. It may be added that if we assume that Chrétien and his successors thought the thighs symbolical of sex, they may have thought sex itself symbolical. Or (to put it less in our modern phrases) that if the wound was to be a wound in virility, it was to be a wound in the whole virility, spiritual as well as physical. We must not force his imagination so far as to say he did, but we can hardly limit it so far as to say he did not. If it were not he, but we, who add the interpretation, then again we should be prepared to take it in its fullest sense.

(ii) The second comment refers to the lance and the grail. Where Chrétien got these from, or whether he got them from anywhere, we do not know. What seems to be true is that these two things are different in kind from what preceded them. There had been (the scholars tell us) Celtic lances that flamed, but there was no Celtic lance that bled. There had been (they also tell us) vessels and cauldrons which produced physical food ; but the grail in Chrétien did not produce physical food. The whole and exact point of its use was that it provided a substitute for physical food. Perceval and the knights and the Fisher King are served with supper ; but the question Perceval did not ask was : ' What serves the Grail ? ' It served an unknown personage with a Host ; if it was like anything, it was like the ciborium of the Eucharist, and contained the super-substantial food.

(iii) The third point is no more than the suggestion of a possibility. It will be remarked that there were two reasons given for Perceval's failure to ask the question : (i) the advice of Gournemant, (ii) his state of sin consequent on his treatment of his mother. It a little looks as if Chrétien, in writing, had felt that the first was inadequate and had strengthened it by the second. A question of such importance, it might be held, ought to have been prevented by some matter more grave than the

A.T.   F

61

misapplication of an old man's maxims. It is, of course, possible
that the first reason was that which Perceval's conscious mind
supplied and that the second—the sense of guilt precluding an
enquiry into apparent sanctity—was the real motive, and that
Chrétien meant it so. He would not have talked in those terms
but he need not have been ignorant of such facts. The main
point is that Perceval's respect for Gournemant is too small a
cause for so heavy a result, even allowing that Gournemant was
Perceval's father in chivalry, to whom special honour was owed.
But the death of the lady his mother is due to a breach in a filial
relationship of blood and not of knighthood ; he has shown a
callous impatience in not returning when he saw her swoon.
However proper his impulse to go, it is credible that the manner
of it should involve him in sin ; and it is certainly credible that,
being so involved, he should not be able to ask concerning a
holy thing. There is the first faint hint—it is no more and is
probably unintentional—of a natural but unhallowed impulse
which fails before holiness.

The poets who followed and continued Chrétien took full
advantage of his themes. All that is necessary here is to relate
certain things in them to the development of the myth as it
later crossed into England and became known to the general
reader.

(i) The first of these is the nature of the vessel itself. In the
continuation the indefinite article is changed to the definite. ' A
grail ' becomes ' the Grail ' and presently ' le Saint Graal ' or
' the Holy Grail '. It is said in so many words to be that which
received the blood of Christ when he was on the cross, and the
Bleeding Lance is said to be the spear of the centurion Longinus
which he thrust into the side of Christ. These identifications
mean that the Sacred Body enters into and becomes a part of
the tale. It is not, at present, much more ; there are hardly any
theological attributions. But poetically there is now a union
and a centre—not so much a Christian centre as an artistic.
From this poetic point of view, the whole development of the
myth is a kind of working out of a theme which is eventually

discovered to be the Christian theme. The centurion was extremely convenient; there he was, complete with spear and action. It is obvious that he was a poetic gift; he had not yet been used, and no poet (once the episode had occurred to him) could think of neglecting him. The general decision of scholars seems to be that none of the Continuators are likely to have had more than plain narrative in mind. But even plain narrative is the better for the unifying and heightening of its images. The Grail, therefore, was identified; it was also released. It was seen, or rather that light more than many candles which accompanied it, was seen outside the castle. Perceval sees it by night in that vast and ancient forest which surrounds the high cities of the myth; it is carried by its maiden or by an angel. It moves in Logres at the will of its keepers—or perhaps at its own will, but I think this has not yet happened. All of this, however, is a preparation for the later time when, in the English Malory, it was to be seen at Pentecost, veiled, before all the Table. It is also for the healing of wounds; when Perceval has fought with Sir Ector, it heals them both. On the other hand, it cannot—or at least does not—heal the Wounded Fisher-King. Nor does it restore fertility to the land outside the castle. In Chrétien this is not yet waste; only through Perceval's silence, some great good that might have come to it does not come. In the continuations, however, the land is already sterile, and the Grail does not restore it without that human initiative which the question implies. The holy thing (' chose espirituelle ') cannot or will not nourish either its keeper or the earth until the called and choosing knight is there.

(ii) But even when the waste land had been supplied, and therefore the great good defined, the cause of the sterility and of the wound of the Fisher-King was still lacking. The important invention here was the first hint of the Dolorous Blow. In one of the continuations Perceval does ask the question, but no healing immediately follows. The Fisher-King tells him that he has been wounded by a sword (not, here, a spear) that has also slain his brother; he can only be healed when the murderer himself has been killed. In fact Perceval presently does slay the murderer and brings his head to the castle, whereupon the king, with a great cry, is made whole. But neither the original blow nor the healing seem yet related directly to the Grail. As for the sword which struck the blow, this is one of the various strange swords which wander in and out of the tale, but again without any apparent direct relation to the central Hallows. There is no need to follow them here ; there is a possible relation, but that can be better discussed later. Perceval left the castle and returned to the court of King Arthur. In one continuation, however, he was called back. The Grail-bearing maiden herself came to the court and told him that the Fisher-King was dead. He had been said to be another uncle of Perceval, so that by now Perceval himself has been raised to be part of the dynasty entrusted with the Guardianship and his relations are hermits and strange wardens. Perceval set out for the castle, but this time the king himself and all the chivalry accompanied him. It is but an episode in one poem, but prophetic of what is happening to the myth. The great Arthurian tradition is already beginning to move towards this other centre. On the Feast of All Saints Perceval was crowned king. King Arthur and the lords remained for a month in the castle where, under the influence of the Grail, they were fed with the richest food. Nothing more is heard of that other more ancient king who was in seclusion and fed only by the Host. King Arthur returned to Britain or Logres, and Perceval reigned for seven years. After that time he left the castle for a hermitage where the Hallows accompanied him. There he was after five years made a priest, and there, fed by the Grail—but now spiritually—he remained till he died. This was afterwards to remain his end in the myth ; after the ascension of Galahad, ' Sir Percivale ', says Malory, ' yielded him to a hermitage out of the city, and took a religious clothing. . . . Thus a year and two months lived Sir Percivale in the hermitage a full holy life, and then passed out of this world ; and Bors let bury him by his sister and by Galahad in the spiritualities.'

(iii) The mention of ' his sister ' raises another point—of the women related to Perceval in the beginnings. There are three, Blanchfleur and the Lady of the Chessboard and his sister. Blanchfleur was the young chatelaine of Beaurepair, the niece of Gournemant, whom he had delivered from her enemy and with whom for a night he had slept. It was a sleep of betrothal rather than of casualness ; they promised marriage in the morning, and are bound. But after that—in one poem—he had a strange adventure in a castle where he played chess with an invisible opponent and met a lady who promised him her love if he would kill a certain stag (the chase of such a stag by one or other champion is a common episode). Eventually he did so, and returned to take his pleasure with the lady. But in another continuation, which does not trouble about the chessboard, it was Blanchfleur to whom he returned in the end, but they proposed to themselves, though they lay side by side, to indulge no intercourse with each other until the adventures of the Grail were ended. There came, however, presently a voice from heaven which encouraged them not to abandon their ' delit carnel ', and prophesied that from that marriage should spring Godfrey of Bouillon, the conqueror of Jerusalem.[1]

But this dedication obviously puts Blanchfleur in at least indirect relation with the Grail. Unfortunately at that point she disappears from the story for the time. She is, however, by now a kind of assistant in the grand adventure, as is the third lady his sister. No sister had been heard of in Chrétien ; the only lady there of Perceval's kin was his mother. But in one of the continuations he returns to his mother's house and there finds his sister, ' blanc cum floure en may novele '. She visits with him the hermit-uncle ; they pray together ; they hear a Mass of the Holy Ghost. He is encouraged and commanded to the adventure. It is to be feared that the Lady of the Chessboard ruined Perceval's chances—but perhaps they were not high—of being the final Grail hero, for reasons which we shall see. One cannot wholly separate a mythical hero from his past in the myth.

[1] Also the Swan Knight of another tale, but he cannot be followed here. [C. W.]

But there remained that figure of sanctity, feminine and self-giving, ' une sainte chose ', who in Malory gave her blood for another and whose dead body was carried to the final achievement on the deck of that ship where were Bors, and Percivale and Galahad—to be buried in ' the spiritual places '.

It may be remarked that in these poems Gawaine plays a part, but never much of a part as regards the Grail. He does reach the castle, but he falls asleep there ; he is a great lord, but he had been (I suspect) too much a great lord of the court. Something simpler and stranger was needed. The result, however, was that, as the court and the Grail drew together, Gawaine lost place. He had no intense relation either to the Sacred Body or to the body of the queen.

But all these developments and variations left one part of the myth yet untold—the early history of the holy thing. De Borron set out to supply this ; he said he had it ' from the great book in which are the histories told by the grand clerks ; there the mighty secrets are written which are named and called the Grail '. Some account of this part of the tale must be given here.

After the arrest of Christ, the vessel in which he made his sacrament—' ou Criz faisoit son sacrament ', ' la senefiance de ma mort '—was found in the house and taken to Pilate. Pilate, wishing to be free from all connexion with him, gave it to Joseph of Arimathea at the time he came to beg the Sacred Body. When the Body was taken from the Cross and bathed, the wounds began again to bleed. Joseph caught the blood in the vessel and hid it in his own house, as he did the body in the tomb. After the harrowing of hell and the resurrection, Joseph was seized and imprisoned by the Jews in a tall tower which could be entered only from the top. There our Lord appeared to him, himself bringing the Grail, from which light shone, and deigned to declare himself concerning it. It is to have three keepers ; all who see it will be of the Lord's own company, and shall have the desire of their hearts, and perdurable joy ; those who can understand these words will not, if they are true

men, ever be defrauded or falsely judged in any court or defeated
in ordeal of battle. The sacrament will never be celebrated
without recollection of Joseph, because of the tenderness and
care he has shown for the body of Christ ; and in those celebra-
tions the elements will be indeed his flesh and blood ; [1] the cup
will represent the Grail and be called a chalice ; the altar is the
tomb ; the corporal the grave clothes ; the paten the stone at
the mouth of the tomb. There is then communicated to Joseph
the secret which is the Grail. Christ leaves the actual Grail with
him and vanishes. Joseph remained in prison for forty years,
fed by the sacred vessel.

At the end of that time the Emperor of Rome and his son
Vespasian come to Jerusalem. Vespasian had been a leper and
had been healed by the handkerchief of Veronica. He and his
father intended to avenge the death of Christ ; and Vespasian
himself, on hearing of Joseph from the Jews, descended into the
tower and set the prisoner free. Once released, Joseph gathered
a company of believers round him and set out on a great journey ;
among them were his sister Enygeus and her husband Hebron
or Bron. They travelled a long distance to the west ; but
presently they settled in a certain district and gave themselves
to prayer and the cultivation of the earth. Some of them, however, fell into sin, and the land itself began to become sterile.
Joseph prayed before the Grail for direction, and a voice from
the Holy Ghost told him what he must do.

He made, at these commands, a great table, such as that was
at which Christ made the significance of his death. One seat
was to be drawn back from it, in memory of Judas, and left
unfilled until the son of Bron should at some future time sit
there. Bron was sent to catch a fish and it was laid on the
table, where also the Grail was set, but covered. The whole
company were called in and invited to sit down. Some did,
but some did not. Those who did were filled with a divine
sweetness ; they experienced the satisfaction of all desire. Those

---

[1] It will be remembered that He was—and is—believed to be received perfect
and entire under either species. [C. W.]

who could not sit felt nothing; these were the sinners. These were sent away, but one of them, Moyses, after many entreaties, made an effort to sit down in the withdrawn and perilous chair. The earth at once opened and swallowed him; there, the sacred voice proclaimed, he must be left until he who was meant for the chair shall come. This was the wrath of the Grail.

Presently the true company were given more commands. Bron and his wife had twelve children, of whom the youngest Alain was to be the father of another Alain, who should become the third keeper of the Grail. The second was to be Bron himself, and it was now the time for the Grail to be delivered to him. Alain was sent away with a part of the company to preach Christ among the heathen. But Joseph in a high ceremony gave the holy vessel into the guardianship of Bron, who by divine instruction was henceforth to be called the Rich Fisher; to him also the secrets were communicated. The Fisher also went on with the rest of the company, carrying the Grail and passing to the West. But there, wherever he chose, he might remain until his son's son should come—to whom the vessel and the grace should pass. Arimathean Joseph remained in his own land, celestially blest. The mystery that lies behind all is his care for that arch-natural Body, when he took it from the cross. It is that deposition which, in some sense, governs all the myth; and this which lies behind the future rejection of Lancelot. It was for that reason that there had been made known to Joseph in his prison 'the holy words, sweet and precious, gracious and pitiful, which are called the Secret of the Grail'. It is added, in the prose version, that those who hear are entreated to ask no more, for anyone who should say more would only lie, and the lie would be without profit, for the truth could not be told. Something of it was to be shown in the mystical chastity and the single wholeness of Galahad.

The poem now says that it would be proper to tell of the adventures of the companies, but that shall not yet be, for another branch is to be followed first. This is to be the tale of Merlin.

The Coming of the Grail

That last figure of sacred magic, of magic before magic even in art became impermissible, lay to his hand,[1] and he found it—fortunate, and we also. Merlin in this was to be a prophet of the Grail. It was a moment of high poetic alteration. De Borron added here another ancient book to those many of which we have heard in these poems. For he pretended that the hermit to whom Merlin's mother had gone in her distress—he perhaps of whom Layamon had written—was entreated by Merlin to write down the history of these things, and this at first he hesitated to do lest it should lead to sin, but reassured by the wizard, he consented. First he wrote the ancient history of the Grail, and then he turned to Merlin's own life. It is said that the Keepers of the Grail were now in North Britain, and that Blaise was there also.

The tale of his birth, of his coming to Uther Pendragon and of the birth of Arthur, has been given. A great theology was entering the myth. The story of the Round Table was already in existence, but de Borron, if he knew of it, would have nothing of so ordinary a convenience merely for civil peace. The First Table (Merlin said) had been established by Christ himself; the Second by Joseph of Arimathea, at the bidding of Christ himself; the Third was to be by Uther, at the bidding of Merlin. This alteration gives the myth a new stress, for the idea of a spiritual relationship is immediately present, circles of sanctity. The Apostolic company is the first institution ; the company of true believers the second ; the third is the chivalry of the Table. At the first is our Lord ; at the second the fish caught by Bron which was the image of our Lord in the imagination of the young Church,[2] and also the covered vessel of the arch-natural Body and Blood ; at the third there is yet nothing, but something is to be. Logres and the Grail are to come together, and the king is to preside at the union. The empty chair—the Siege Perilous

---

[1] Sc. de Borron's. [C. S. L.]

[2] Ἰχθύς (*fish*) was so used because the initial letters of Ἰησοῦς Χριστὸς Θεοῦ Υἱὸς Σωτήρ (*Iesus CHristos THeou Uios Soter*—Jesus Christ, Son of God, Saviour) make up Ἰχθύς (*ichthus*). [C. S. L.]

—is to be left there also till he who was to be the union should come. He was to sit, as it were, in the seat of Judas—and of Moyses—so making up the number of the elect. The Table is to be set up by Uther at Cardoil in Wales, but it is Caerleon which presently seems to stand for the city of Arthur on those far frontiers, near (as it must seem to be) to Broceliande and all that the myth should show living in Carbonek.

There is, however, another poem called *Perlesvaux*, which some suppose to be an early and some a late text. It was translated into English in the nineteenth century by Sebastian Evans. He was a poet of a certain power, though his medievalism is of the usual mannered and slightly picturesque kind common to that period ; if not pre-Raphaelite it is at least kindred to that manner. But this matters less perhaps in a poem of this kind than it might in some medieval texts. And even Wardour Street (though I do not think that Sebastian Evans lived in or anywhere near Wardour Street) is a less falsifying street to read in than—as one might say—certain Athenaeums of the mind. A distinguished modern scholar, writing of Perceval's association with some young woman in a castle, speaks of his ' asceticism ' in not going to bed with her. ' Asceticism ' is a grand word to use for a mere refusal of fornication. Another modern writer says : ' There is more practical moral teaching in Chrétien's Percival than in all the Galahad romances put together.' If this were true—which I do not believe—it would be because the Galahad romances had a greater and more inclusive imagination, and took the moral teaching largely for granted. The figure of the High Prince is for something much more than morals. The Victorians, in spite of the morality attributed to them, did not make these particular mistakes. Tennyson's figure of Galahad is highly inadequate, but its inadequacy is relevant to the original whereas many of the commentators' remarks are not.

The *High History* is the fullest Perceval romance. It does not entirely unite the Arthur theme and the Grail theme, and this is the more disappointing because it starts off as if it were going to do precisely that ; in fact, the opening is very fine and worthy of a greater supernatural story than the *High History*. It is almost the only, if not indeed the only, romance in which the king is himself involved in the visions. Arthur had grown slothful in majesty, to the loss of his reputation and to the distress of Queen Guinevere. This seems, in some sense, to correspond with the unasked question, the lethargy of King Arthur and the languishment of King Fisherman (as he is called here) being of the same kind but in different orders. When King Arthur, to begin to recover his fame, rode out alone on adventure he came to a hermitage where was the dead body of the hermit, and there he heard the voice of Our Lady rebuking the devils and gathering to her the soul of the dead man. In the chapel of another hermit-age into which he was not permitted to enter, he saw something of the mystery of the Eucharist. First he saw a very fair woman sitting by the altar with a child on her knee. She gave the child into the hands of the hermit, but when he ' began his sacrament ' the king saw that he held not a child but a man bleeding and thorn-crowned. King Arthur ' seeth him in his own figure . . . and hath pity of him in his heart that he hath seen, and the tears come into his eyes '. A bright light shines ; presently the man is changed again to the child ; and finally at the voice of an angel crying : ' *Ite : missa est* ', the Son and his Mother vanish from the chapel, with ' the fairest company that might ever be seen ', and the light ceases. Afterwards he is told of King Fisherman, the Grail, and the unasked question, and how for want of the question ' all the lands are commoved to war '. Human brotherhood, in fact, has been broken. This is a sug-gestion of wider scope than the ruin or sterility of the land directly associated with the Castle contains, but it is not further worked out. The king was told also of the Good Knight Perlesvaux, of how his widow mother has been attacked by the Lord of the Moors, and how search is being made for Perlesvaux, or Percival, since only he can aid his mother and heal the dis-tresses of the lands. After hearing of these things, King Arthur returns to Cardoil where he promises Guinevere that he will obey our Saviour's will ; ' " for never had none better desire of well-doing than have I at this time, nor of honour nor of largesse." " Sir," saith she, " God be praised thereof." '

With the exception of the actual coming of Galahad to the court of Arthur in Malory, and the appearance of the veiled Cup, this is the nearest in any of the tales that the king himself comes to the mystery. But in neither this version nor in Malory is he taken farther into it. It is the more disappointing here because he has been allowed to ride out on adventure, and because his own better-doing is intimately connected with both the Eucharist and with King Fisherman. One cannot perhaps say that his interest in the mystery flags, but certainly it seems as if the author is only spasmodically concerned to maintain that interest. The book in fact follows two themes—the Grail theme and the Court theme—and the relation between them is not very close. Other inventions were necessary for that.

Some things, however, are common to both, and of these the most important is the conflict everywhere between ' the old law ' and ' the new law '. The first is paganism ; the second, Christianity. But it is the other phrases which are habitually used ; and the expression of ' the new law ' is in the images of our Lord and his Mother and the Hallows. Its centre, in this story, is the Castle of the Hallows which is also called Eden, the Castle of Joy, and the Castle of Souls. But there is also an indication that this is not the final state ; it is, in its own way, the opening and not the conclusion of the true spiritual knowledge. In the end Perceval himself leaves it and goes to a hermitage in the forest, and the Grail accompanies him.

Perceval is throughout the champion and great master for whose adequate coming everything waits, and this though he himself has been first responsible for the unasked question. He was the son of Alain le Gros—of the lineage of Joseph of Abarimacie—the lord of the Valleys of Camelot. But this Camelot is not King Arthur's ; it ' stood upon the uttermost headland of the wildest isle of Wales by the sea to the West. Nought was there save the hold and the forest and the waters that were round about it. The other Camelot, that was King Arthur's, was situate at the entrance of the kingdom of Logres, and was peopled of folk and was seated at the head of the King's land, for that he had in his governance all the lands that on that side marched with his own.' One cannot say more of this duplication of the name than that it is a duplication and a contrast. One must not symbolically identify them. But at least one may admit that, in reading, an echo passes from one to the other ; and the well-populated city of the king remotely opens upon the solitary hold of the Widow Lady on the uttermost headland of the wildest isle with only the forest and the waters about it. She had three brothers : King Fisherman who kept the Grail in the Castle of Souls ; King Pelles, who had left his crown and become one of the hermits of whom the high strange forest is full ; and the King of Castle Mortal, who has turned to evil, robbed his sister of her inheritance, and is determined to seize on the Grail Castle itself—which indeed, after the death of King Fisherman, he does. It is in the forest that lies, as it were, between the two Camelots that most of the adventures pass. The hermitages are there, with their wise and holy dwellers, ' youthful of seeming, because they serve King Fisherman, and the sweetness of that service is so great that a year seems but a month '. Pageants of mysterious damsels go about it ; and knights of one law or of the other ; and the coming out of it is towards one Camelot or the other, though Perceval and Gawaine and Lancelot and the king ride through it and know both ends.

Gawaine indeed is in this version allowed more than he is given elsewhere. After the opening adventures, the king in the pursuit of well-doing holds ' a high-plenary court ' ; this, in such a romance, is the business of honour and largesse. Gawaine is there engaged to go to King Fisherman ; but when he does so —finding the castle full of chapels, priests, and ancient knights, and in the chief chapel ' the service of the most holy Grail '—he is told by the king that he cannot hope to enter until he brings with him the sword with which St. John Baptist was beheaded, now in the possession of a pagan king. The possession of this he eventually achieves, and brings it to the Fisherman. He is warned again to remember to ask the question. The pageant appears ; one damsel carries the Grail and another the Lance, the point of which bleeds into the Grail. Gawaine ' is thoughtful, and so great a joy cometh to him that naught remembereth he in his thinking save God only '. He seems to see three damsels where he had seen but two and in the midst of the Grail the figure of a child ; afterwards, still among the seeming three damsels, he sees ' the Grail all in flesh, and he seeth above, as him thinketh, a King crowned, nailed upon a rood, and the spear was still fast in his side. Messire Gawaine seeth it and hath great pity thereof, and of nought doth he remember him save of the pain that this King suffereth.' He therefore fails to ask the question, for when the knights and the Master of the knights look and call to him, he remains unconscious of them. ' For the first and only time recorded of him in all the literature, the thought of God overflows his whole consciousness.' [1] He is therefore on the next day compelled to leave the castle, and the dolours remain unhealed.

The achievement of Perceval is a much longer business and has unusual variations. The death of King Fisherman and the seizure of the castle by the King of Castle Mortal are among these. No particular significance in this seems to be suggested ; the Grail and the Hallows withdraw at the moment of the conquest and do not manifest again till Perceval comes. He is much more spiritually related to his mother the Widow Lady and his sister Dindrane, and they to the mysteries. Dindrane's own adventure in the Graveyard . . .[2]

What then is the Achievement of the Grail ? Dante, in a later century, was to put the height of human beatitude in the

---

[1] A. E. Waite : *The Hidden Church of the Holy Grail.*

[2] The sentence is incomplete. In my opinion all that follows probably made part of a separate chapter and there is probably a long hiatus. Others, at least as well qualified as I to judge, think differently. [C. S. L.]

understanding of the Incarnation ; in a lesser, but related, method Angela of Foligno was to speak of knowing ' how God comes into the Sacrament '. To know these things is to be native to them ; to live in the world where the Incarnation and the Sacrament (single or multiple) happen. It is more : it is, in some sense, to live beyond them, or rather (since that might sound profane) to be conscious of them as one is conscious of oneself, Christ-conscious instead of self-conscious. The achievement of the Grail is the perfect fulfilment of this, the thing happening.

It is to the French poets and romancers that we owe the bringing of this high myth into relation with Arthur, King of Britain or Logres ; as it is to Geoffrey of Monmouth that we owe the development of the figure of Arthur the king out of the doubtful records of the Captain-General of Britain ; and as we owe to Sir Thomas Malory the most complete version of the whole in the English language. Much was modified and much added by others. It is perhaps worth while to reshape the whole tale here once more.[1] But we cannot go back behind the royalty which Geoffrey invented. No one can ever uncrown Arthur. The king may have—and indeed must have—the qualities of the Captain-General, but he must be the king.

At a time then when the Roman and Christian civilization in Britain was seriously endangered by the invasions of the pirate and pagan forces, there arose a patriotic movement of considerable force. It was at first led by Aurelius Ambrosius, of a noble Romano-British family ; after his death, his brother Uther, called Pendragon, succeeded to the leadership and by his victories was named for a brief period king of all Britain. He was the father—canonically, but with some strangeness about the birth—of a son, Arthur. At that time the centre of the Roman *imperium* lay in Byzantium. The Empire was Christian, and not only Christian but orthodox and Trinitarian. The Arian heresies had

---

[1] Here the history of the earlier legends ends. What follows describes the growth of the legend in Charles Williams's own mind into the form it has in his poems and was to have in his unwritten poems. [C. S. L.]

been defeated. Christ was adored as God and not as a created being. The variations of this which were called Nestorianism had also been overcome.[1] It had been determined that the mystery of redemption lay not only in the operation of true God but by that operation in flesh and blood. It was generally accepted, though not yet defined, that the Incarnacy deigned to maintain Himself (in His Passion and Resurrection) in His Eucharists. The Pope was in possession of Rome ; about both his figure and that of the remote Emperor in Byzantium there lay something of a supernatural light—at best mystical, at worst magical. There was, for all disputes between East and West, as yet no great schism in Christendom. The prince Arthur grew to youth in that Catholic world ; and this is, eastward from Logres, the condition of his life and reign. But as this is the historic relation, so on the other—westward from Logres—there is the mythical. In a sense, of course, history is itself a myth ; to the imaginative, engaged in considering these things, all is equally myth. We may issue from it into other judgements— doctrinal, moral, historic. But so doing we enter into another kind of thought and judge by other tests—more important perhaps, but not the same. In the myth we need ask for nothing but interior consistency ; thus, if we choose to have it so, there is no reason why Julius Caesar should not hear the souls of the dead putting off in spectral boats from the shores of Gaul. There is no reason why Camus and St. Peter should not both lament Lycidas (for whom, after all, rather than Edward King, Milton supposed himself to be sorrowing. But Edward King *is* Lycidas ? it is certain that Lycidas is something more than Edward King). It is in an ocean where such tales are relevant that Britain lies ; that is why it is Logres, which is Britain in an enlarging world— Britain and more than Britain. It is more like that mysterious Albion of which Blake wrote in another geography.

There lie then near Logres—and they must lie to the west, for to the east we come into history and doctrine and Europe—

[1] It is possible that Charles Williams intended to mention more than one heresy, but the text, as it stands, can be defended. [C. S. L.]

other places of the myth. There is the mysterious forest of Broceliande : there are the seas on which the ship of Solomon is to sail ; beyond them is Sarras. It is certainly true that Sarras was originally on the borders of Egypt, but that cannot now be helped, for the lords of the Quest must go there in a ship, and it must lie beyond Carbonek. To send the ship back from Carbonek through the Mediterranean to Egypt—I will not say it could not be done, for anything can be done that can be done, but it seems less convenient than to remove Sarras ; especially as Sarras can be spiritually reached anywhere, but it is not quite suitable that the High Prince should return to the world. He who does that is Bors.

Carbonek itself must be, if not in, at least on the borders of Broceliande. It is the castle of the Hallows ; there are in its chapel the Grail and the Spear. The Spear is that which pierced the heart of Christ ; the Grail is the vessel used at the Last Supper, in which also the blood from the wounded heart was caught. The Keeper of the Castle is the King Pelles, and in the processions of the Grail it is carried by his daughter Helayne. She is maiden, and all but vowed to maidenhood ; only there lies over her the rejection of that desired life ; she is to be the mother of the Grail-lord. It would be perhaps a pity to lose from the tale the other name of Castle Mortal and its king ; but if it is to be kept, there is only one figure who can occupy it, and that is the brother of Pelles, the invisible knight, who is called Garlon. That castle too must stand in Broceliande.

It is indeed in that forest, inextricably mingled with the mystical sea spiritual distance,[1] that all these places of marvel must lie. It is, after all, one of the great forests of myth— greater because of its hidden mysteries than Arden or Birnam or Westermain. The wood of Comus may be compared with it ; and indeed is poetically a part of it, except that it is a holy place and uninhabited by such sorcerers. But some of the outlying parts might be given up to him—until the Judgement. A nobler comparison is with that forest which Dante found at the

---

[1] ' Sea spiritual ' (or ' sea-spiritual ') is, I think an adjective. [C. S. L.]

A.T.   G

foot of the Mount of Purgatory and where he came again to himself, or that other on the height of the Mount where Beatrice came again to him. But it is not proper to do more than shyly observe comparisons between such myths. It is a place of making and of all the figures concerned with making.

Of these one of the most mysterious is Nimue, the Lady of the Lake. Swinburne's great description of her is too effective to be lost. Tennyson turned her into a kind of allegory of the Church, and (if baptism were involved) this might be well enough. But of the two Swinburne's is the greater, for the ecclesiastical and religious figures are already patterned, and the High Prince himself has his own Way, not to be confused. So that Nimue is the great mother and lady of Broceliande—Nature, as it were, or all the vast processes of the universe imaged in a single figure.

There is, however, a problem about Merlin. He is so very much a preparation for the Grail that his earlier diabolic birth seems almost improper to so high a vocation, though it might be worked in well enough. On the other hand there is something attractive in a small invention which would be inconsistent with this diabolic conception. The central fact of the conception of Galahad depends partly on the strange drink given to Lancelot by Brisen, the nurse of Helayne. She in fact prepares within Carbonek what Merlin prophesies and prepares (by his calling of Arthur) in Logres. It might be permissible to make them twins, children of some high parthenogenetical birth of Nimue in Broceliande. They would come then almost like Time and Place to their mission, to prepare in Carbonek and Camelot for the moment of the work.

The calling of Arthur, and the freeing of Logres (or Britain) from the pagans and tyrants is the first movement of the mystery. The Matter of Britain begins with this, leading to the coronation of the king; when, in the old phrase, ' he put on his crown '. What, however, obviously ought not to happen, and what in Malory and Tennyson is already an almost minor episode, is his war against the Emperor. This was very well in the chivalric battles of Geoffrey, though Nationalism (too often attributed only to the Renascence) is already there getting slightly out of hand. But a kind of supreme wordly glory is Arthur's climax. Even then—by accident or design—he was never allowed to meet the Emperor in battle, and all that Tennyson says is that ' Arthur strove with Rome '. It had better be dropped. No national myth was ever the better for being set against a more universal authority—in our own day we have learnt that—though it might be desirable to heighten the *imperium* in order conveniently to include this royalty within it. But in a myth Byzantium may be many things. It may also be urged, for what the point is worth, that it was in fact this Roman and universal authority for which, in however shadowy a way, the historic Arthur was fighting against the barbarians ; it is not for him himself to fight against it. Nor, now, to win conquests over other nations as such. He is a champion, not a conquistador.

It is in fact here that the centre of the myth must be determined. The problem is simple—is the king to be there for the sake of the Grail or not ? It was so the Middle Ages left it ; but since then it has been taken the other way. The Grail has been an episode. This may still be so, but it can no longer be accidentally so. Tennyson, in that sense, was right ; he meant to make the Grail an episode, and he did. He said it was only for certain people, and he modified the legend accordingly. If it is to be more, it must take the central place. Logres then must be meant for the Grail. (There is a difficulty here about the Dolorous Blow which may be mentioned in a moment.) This indeed must be the pure glory of Arthur and Logres. Vessels of plenty have nothing to do with it ; were it true (as it is not) that the Grail had developed from them, it would still have developed out of all common measurement. It is the central matter of the Matter of Britain. We may, if we choose, reasonably and properly refuse it, but we can hardly doubt that if we do we shall have no doubt a consistent, but a much smaller myth.

For the Grail, so understood, must itself be—I will not say enlarged, for that is impossible, but it must be understood in all its meanings and relationships. It is the tale of Galahad ; it is the tale of the mystical way ; but also it is the tale of the universal way. It is not, as in Tennyson, only for the elect ; it is for all. It is in this sense that the three lords of the Quest are of importance. Bors is in the chapel at Sarras as well as Galahad and Percivale. This is what relates the Achievement to every man. The tale must end, and that part of it when the holy thing returns again to earth—when Galahad is effectually in Bors as Bors is implicitly in Galahad—cannot be told until the clause of the Lord's prayer is fulfilled and the kingdom of heaven is come upon earth, perhaps not until there is a new heaven and a new earth. It must therefore vanish : and Bors must return —in spite of the fact that there are hints, even in Malory, that the mere passage of the Grail destroyed the kingdom. Since the *Grand St. Graal* nothing has ever been quite the same. That romance worked on the literature the effect which the Grail worked on Logres. The only question is whether that work is a necessary part of the Achievement.

If then the Grail is to be fully accepted, in every sense, it must be accepted from the beginning. I have sometimes thought that the best way would be to imagine that Logres was designed to be a place for the coming of the Grail. The immediate expectation of the Second Coming had faded, but the vision of it remained as it has always remained in the Church. It might be taken that the King Pelles, the Keeper of the Hallows, was at the proper time, when Merlin had brought Arthur into his royalty and Logres had been cleared and established, to emerge from Carbonek into Logres, directing the processions of the Grail and the prelude of the Second Coming. Logres was to be blessed thus, and he who said Mass in Sarras would say it in Caerleon and Camelot as he did in Jerusalem. This, however, is but one means to making the tale coherent, and need not be pressed. The more urgent problems are the place of the unasked question and of the Dolorous Blow. They are, of course, strictly speaking, alternatives. It is certain that we must keep the Dolorous Blow ; a loss of that would mean a loss of the Wounded King, which cannot be imagined. The only question is whether we can have the unasked question also.

It would not be impossible, if the whole thing were regarded as a tale of the Fall—individual or universal. The union would be in the fact that the lack of the question would mean the lack of an answer, and hence an ignorance of the true nature of the Invisible Knight. This was one of the secrets Gawaine should have learned and reported ; not learning and not reporting, he left the Court ignorant and Balin the Savage free to avenge his host's son. The refusal to ask the question is precisely that refusal to inquire which accompanies so many a temptation and encourages so many a sin. 'What serves the Grail ?' The answer is ' You and all Logres '. It is not so much the encouragement of a sin that is so often sinful as a refusal to encourage the counter-movement, the opposite of a sin. After that, the ignorant savage is free.

The Dolorous Blow consisted in the wounding of the royal Keeper of the Hallows with the Sacred Spear. The Spear was that which had wounded the side of Christ, and it bled continually at the point. It was then aimed at the central heart. But when Balin le Sauvage used it, he used it for his own self-preservation. It is this turning of the most sacred mysteries to the immediate security of the self that is the catastrophic thing. It is indeed, morally, precisely the wounding of the Keeper of the Hallows which then takes place. Man wounds himself. It is an image of the Fall ; it is also an image of every individual and deliberate act of malice, though the deliberation is here but passionate and not coldly angry.

It has, of course, every excuse. The mystery of the Invisible Knight—say, the Invisible Slayer—is abroad in the world. He might have been explained, had the question been asked. As it is, he rides destructively, but in the hall of Carbonek he is at last seen and known ; it may be that even there he was a dark knight, and perhaps the King or Duke of Castle Mortal, since one must not over-multiply the title of king. There is here a certain similitude to the figure of the Holy Ghost, as It exercises Its operations in the world. For Balin actually to kill an inhabitant of Broceliande can hardly be allowed : the forest and its people are not of a kind that could be overcome in that manner. But the ever-bleeding wound of the Keeper is exactly symbolical, and so is the ruin that falls on Logres. A new darkness and sterility begin to creep through the land from which the pagans have been expelled. The outer conquests are not the inner. Victory is being still celebrated in Camelot when defeat issues from Carbonek.

This, even in the direct incidents of the tale, is not an exaggeration. One incident is directly the consequence of the Dolorous Blow ; and there is another like it which should be. The first is that Balin the Savage in ignorance kills his own brother Balan, and Balan him. The natural pieties begin to be lost, and there is incivility in the blood. It is in fact the farther externalization of the Wounded King. But the disorder spreads farther. In the first tales Mordred was the king's nephew ; in later versions he became the king's son by incest, but unknown incest. The queen Morgause of Orkney, the wife of King Lot, was Arthur's sister. But he does not know this when she comes to his court, and he tempts her to lie with him. The birth of that incestuous union is Mordred, and the fate of the Round Table comes into the world almost before the Table has been established ; say, at the very feast of the crowning of Arthur and the founding of the Table. The seed of its destroyer lies in the womb of Morgause while she watches the ceremonies. This is not irony ; it is something beyond irony. No doubt the wise young master Merlin knows, but it is not for him to speak, or only in riddles. He knows that the egress of the Grail from Carbonek has now been prevented, but also he prepares the Perilous Seat. He sets that empty chair among all the chairs ; he promises an achievement, and a restoration from a destruction which is known then to him alone.

This now is the double way of Logres, of the Table, and of

the king. The glory of Arthur continues. He marries Guinevere—the most beautiful woman. He has for friend and chief lord Lancelot, the bravest and noblest man. Lancelot is chief in the heart of both the king and the queen. It was a wise instinct that kept the old writers from making Arthur himself a lord in love between a man and a woman. It is the high brotherhood of arms and friendship in which he is noble ; that is his own personal share in the glory of his kingdom. But it is an actual kingdom and an actual glory : that is, Lancelot has his proper duties to the State. The political side of the kingdom is not to be denied or despised, and the Table itself is a part of the settlement. All the champions are still to be champions of the good ; in that Tennyson was right, though he perhaps a little slurred the inevitable dullness of their duty. The Table is a gathering of the realm as well as of knighthood, and if Lancelot is not a Chancellor or Prime Minister he is not unlike. It is observable that in the great parting with Guinevere in Malory he tells her that he would have achieved the Grail ' had not your lord been '. This may refer to the love-conflict, but then one would have expected ' had not you been '. It may again be an error, [1] but if it is not, then it is important. For then we have a definite relation of Lancelot to a more complete way of the Affirmation of Images than has been allowed to him. It is not only to do with a woman, but with men and women ; not only with the queen but with the Republic.

The speech of Sir Ector over the dead Lancelot confirms this. Lancelot, for all the errands upon which he rides, is never merely a knight-errant. He affirms friendship, courtesy, justice, and nobility—in all the references allowed them. He is almost the active centre of that kingdom of which Arthur is, in a sense, the passive. Arthur, of course, is no such poor thing, but it is true he does not *seem* to act.

Lancelot then is the chief figure of the Way of Affirmations.

[1] It almost certainly is. Malory XXI. ix reads *lord*, but Winchester MS. (ed. F. Vinaver, Oxford, 1947, Vol. III, p. 1253) reads *love*. The Winchester text was, of course, inaccessible when Charles Williams wrote. [C. S. L.]

The great Arthuriad is no longer a division between this and its opposite and complementary companion—the Way of Rejections. The tales of Arthur and of the Grail, of Camelot and Carbonek, may have been as antagonistic in their first invention as scholars maintain. They are now no longer so. There is, no doubt, a separation, but the separation is the union ; and this is not so alien from our experience that we need reject in myth what we have to accept in mere living. The moral of the whole is as firm as ever Tennyson would have made it, but it is deeper in its metaphysic.

Between Guinevere and Lancelot there has risen this fatal love—fatal but not fated. No magical potion has been its source, such as Tristram and Iseult drank between sea and sky. The spring, and young blood, and generous hearts, are its beginning. Guinevere has always been a slight difficulty, for in the situation of the tale, she has nothing to do but to be in love with Lancelot. He can ride out, and have adventures, and return, but she can only sit and work at embroideries and love. It is therefore only in relation to that that she has hitherto existed. I suppose something more might be done with her ; her royalty might be stressed in actions. But it has not yet happened. Her phrases are love's phrases—embittered or noble. ' And so I report me unto all the Table Round ', etc. She retains to the end that capacity for stabbing at Lancelot ; it is to be forgiven because of her very great dolour, and because it is not for us to revenge what Lancelot accepted.

I am not sure that, for all Chrétien de Troyes and the others did with it, the great love-tale comes properly now under the heading of Romantic Love, either in the historic or the metaphysical sense. It began certainly with Romance. But Malory, as was said, has made it different. It is the affirmation of one kind of image and not of another. It is certainly not any nonsense of the ' death-wish ' as M. de Rougemont suggests. Malory knows nothing of lovers who desire to perish. Subconsciously ? Nor that ; through all their beings these great lovers desire life, honour, and reciprocal joy. Some such element might—though

I do not much believe it—be felt in the Tristram drink, though in Malory Tristram shows little enough awareness of it. But Lancelot and the queen are simply not of that kind at all. Any more than we are—in spite of our occasional dark indulgence of ourselves in our sorrows.

It is indeed their situation—in life and desire for life—which in Malory offers such profound hints. The soul, affirming the validity of those images which appear to it, finds itself, physically or mentally, caught in its own desire to appropriate them. The temptation of the king—were it stressed, but it is not—would be to be too much himself the State ; to appropriate Logres to himself. The temptation of Lancelot is to appropriate the queen. It is no less a temptation of the soul that it appears as a temptation of the body. It is a temptation of power. Power is not something that one has ; it is something one is. The desire for power is always being thwarted by this misunderstanding. One is not powerful. But if one had x one would be powerful. Power (as Wordsworth showed us) is in one's capacities. The capacities of Lancelot and the queen are distracted.

It is, however, by indirect means that these two great Powers are fulfilled. One must learn to think properly of the personages of the myth, and not less mightily than the names deserve. The Arthuriad recedes into dim forests and seas, and the ship of Solomon driving into the last Mysteries, and in the foreground is a Saracen knight hunting a strange beast which is known by the sound of barking dogs. It is called the Blatant Beast, and when Spenser took it over he turned it into the mob, but it is not that in Malory ; it is only a figure of fable, except that its Paynim pursuer will not be christened till he has overcome it. But he has another quality too, which is his hopeless love for the queen Iseult, but it was Tristram whom she loved and she took no care for Palomides. (And a distinction between ways of thought is between Malory and Austin Dobson's short poem.) These two might well, in some way, be one ; and it is perhaps significant that Palomides is at last christened after his reconciliation with

Tristram (but not with Mark—but of Mark we need say nothing), and that nothing in the end is heard of any seizing of the Blatant Beast.

There is, however, another point where Palomides comes violently into the myth. It is at the famous—and oddly named —Tournament of Lonazep. It is there that Palomides does his greatest deeds—'it is his day', said Sir Dinadan—but also his worst ; for he overthrows Lancelot by falsehood.

www.ingramcontent.com/pod-product-compliance
Lightning Source LLC
Chambersburg PA
CBHW021154090426
42740CB00008B/1079